¡Teatro!

¡Teatro!

Hispanic Plays for Young People

Angel Vigil

1996
Teacher Ideas Press
A Division of
Libraries Unlimited, Inc.
Englewood, Colorado

1463482

I dedicate this book to my wife Sheila.
She is a constant source of support and encouragement.

———

Copyright © 1996 Libraries Unlimited, Inc.
All Rights Reserved
Printed in the United States of America

No part of this publication may be reproduced, stored in a retrieval system, or transmitted, in any form or by any means, electronic, mechanical, photocopying, recording, or otherwise, without the prior written permission of the publisher. An exception is made for individual library media specialists and teachers, who may make copies of activity sheets for classroom use in a single school. Other portions of the book (up to 15 pages) may be copied for in-service programs or other educational programs in a single school.

The plays in this book are fully protected by copyright law. All rights, including motion picture, recitation, radio or television broadcasting, public reading, and rights of translation into foreign languages, are strictly reserved. Productions may not be produced on cable television, videotaped, or otherwise reproduced or transmitted by any electronic or mechanical means, or by any storage or retrieval system, unless written permission and quotation for royalty fees are obtained from Libraries Unlimited, P.O. Box 6633, Englewood, CO 80155-6633, U.S.A.

Permission for performance is granted to schools, clubs, and similar amateur groups without payment of a royalty fee. The individual purchaser of this book may reproduce designated materials in this book for classroom and individual use, but the purchase of this book does not entitle reproduction of any part for an entire school district or system. Such use is strictly prohibited.

All other producers of the scripts in this book must request permission for performance and royalty quotation from Libraries Unlimited.

TEACHER IDEAS PRESS
A Division of
Libraries Unlimited, Inc.
P.O. Box 6633
Englewood, CO 80155-6633
1-800-237-6124

Production Editor: Kevin W. Perizzolo
Copy Editor: Jason Cook
Typesetter: Kay Minnis
Costume Illustrations: Carol Kimball
Graphics: Al Cárdenas

Library of Congress Cataloging-in-Publication Data

Vigil, Angel.
    ¡Teatro! : hispanic plays for young people / Angel Vigil.
    xviii, 169 p. 22x28 cm.
    Includes bibliographical references.
    Summary: Consists of fourteen scripts for classroom use based upon
Hispanic culture and traditions of the American Southwest.
    ISBN 1-56308-371-X
    1. Hispanic Americans--Juvenile drama. 2. Children's plays,
American. [1. Hispanic Americans--Drama. 2. Plays.] I. Title.
PS3572.I338T43   1996
812'.54--dc20
                                                    96-15593
                                                      CIP
                                                       AC

Contents

Part I
Folktales

Part II
Animal Fables

Part III
Holiday Plays

Part IV
An Historical Play

Preface

Folk drama, along with its narrative cousin storytelling, has long served as a central aspect of cultural heritage. The stories that are passed down and the dramatic characters who live in people's imaginations form the foundations upon which a people establish and develop a rich and personal cultural identity. These dramatic traditions contain the folk wisdom and cultural memory that sustain cultural heritage between generations.

The performance of culturally based plays especially enhances the study and experience of a culture's folklore and traditions. Folk drama, often incorporating the rich oral traditions that are at the center of cultural experience, allows students to re-create and directly experience the dramatic characters and events that represent cultural history.

The Hispanic Southwest has a long tradition of folk drama, dating back to the establishment of a Spanish colonial culture in the New World. The Spanish brought with them a rich dramatic tradition dating back to Spain's Golden Age. During the succeeding centuries after the beginning of the Spanish colonization of the American Southwest there existed an active experience of both secular and religious plays. Aurelio Espinosa in his book *The Folklore of Spain in the American Southwest* gives an especially good descriptive overview of the dramatic traditions in the Hispanic Southwest during the Spanish colonial period.

The secular plays were mostly historical plays recounting the battles between the Moors and Christians, as well as plays depicting the encounters with the established Native American cultures. They often presented the history of early colonization and the battles for European cultural supremacy in the New Spanish Empire. The religious plays were based upon European medieval morality and "miracle" plays and biblical events. These plays came directly from Spain or were written by Spanish missionaries in the New World.

The experience of Southwestern Hispanic theatre during the twentieth century is characterized by active growth in both traditional and original expressions of the American Hispanic experience. Such books as Nicolás Kanellos's *Mexican-American Theatre: Then and Now* and Jorge Huerta's *Chicano Theatre: Themes and Forms* discuss the development and practices of Hispanic theatre during the twentieth century in great detail. These books are academic and scholarly in nature and give a good overview of the wide and diverse contributions Hispanic dramatic artists have made in the past and recent decades.

Though Hispanic theatre is a centuries-old experience in the American Southwest, there has not been an abundance of scripts available for educators and youth leaders to perform with young people. Students and teachers at the high school, college, and adult levels are able to produce the historical or modern scripts intended for adult performance. Joe Rosenberg's *¡Aplauso!*, a recently published book, is a welcome addition to the dramatic literature of the field because it is one of the first books to present Hispanic scripts in a collection that contains several plays specifically intended for production by young people.

Several years ago, nationally acclaimed Chicano playwright Carlos Morton and I cowrote the play *Cuentos*, which was produced for the school tour by the Denver Center

Theatre Company. *Cuentos* was based upon the traditional stories and legends of the Hispanic Southwest. Responses to the production from educators were very positive, especially about the unique experience of having culturally based dramatic experiences available for students.

Through the experience of the *Cuentos* production and school tour, it became apparent that the education of elementary and junior high school students could be enriched and enhanced by the availability of culturally based scripts written for this age group. The common refrain from educators was that plays that contributed to the development of cultural education, understanding, and appreciation were not readily available but were greatly needed.

I wrote this book, *Hispanic Plays for Young People*, in response to this expressed desire by educators and youth leaders to have scripts from the Hispanic culture for young people. This book contains a wide variety of plays, to give the educator a diverse set of choices in selecting plays that best fit a particular educational circumstance or goal. By design, the plays are short, simple, and easy to produce. A single play can fill a class period; several plays grouped together would make a wonderful school assembly.

Six plays are based upon folktales of the Hispanic Southwest. I selected these stories because of their strong dramatic situations and interesting, dramatic characters. The stories come from the folktale category, most commonly referred to as stories of transformation, magic, and wonder. Most of the stories are descended from classic European folktales.

Three plays, intended for production by elementary students, are animal fables. These plays present animals as the characters. As in all fables, the story teaches a moral lesson through the adventures of its animal characters. I selected these plays for inclusion in the collection because of the great and easy joy young students find in using their playful and active imaginations when pretending to be animals.

Four plays are based upon cultural holiday celebrations. These plays will help teachers and students enhance the experience and understanding of several Hispanic holiday traditions.

Finally, one play is an historical play based on factual events and historical figures. From the days of Greek drama, through the histories of Shakespeare, to the present time, history has presented the playwright with more than ample drama and powerful characters to populate a stage. This final play is based upon the historical events behind one of the Hispanic Southwest's growing cultural traditions and celebrations, *Cinco de Mayo*.

There are fourteen plays in all. Each play is a dramatic invitation into the heart and soul of the Hispanic culture of the American Southwest. Each play serves as a path for young people to learn about and understand more about one of America's oldest cultures. This book provides a diverse collection of choices for the educator and youth leader, designed to help one choose the plays that best fit one's particular educational circumstances and goals.

Most of all, the plays allow students to directly experience the cultural heritage and wisdom represented in the dramatic events contained within the plays. Through theatre, a dramatic art form based upon the oral and cultural traditions that have developed over centuries of family and personal experience, students, educators, and youth leaders can directly participate in *la cultura hispana*.

Acknowledgments

I wish to thank my publisher, Libraries Unlimited, and my editor at Libraries Unlimited for their support of my work and their commitment to publishing books about the Hispanic culture. Their interest in publishing Hispanic-content books is an important contribution to providing culturally diverse materials for our most important educational markets—schools and libraries.

I also wish to thank two of my long-time collaborators, artists Al Cárdenas and Carol Kimball. Their great talents and willingness to participate in these literary projects continue to bring beauty and artistry to my books. I am very thankful for the opportunity to work with them on a continuing basis.

Introduction

Script Choice

There are fourteen plays in this collection. The plays present a wide range of production choices. This diverse set of options allows the educator and youth leader to choose plays that best fit particular and individual educational circumstances and goals. The table below recommends play choice and production level.

Recommended Production Level

	Lower Elementary (Grades 1-3)	Middle Elementary (Grades 4-6)	Junior High (Grades 6-8)
Folktales			
The Three Pieces of Good Advice		✓	✓
The Most Interesting Gift of All		✓	✓
Blanca Flor, White Flower		✓	✓
El Muchacho que Mato al Gigante, The Boy Who Killed the Giant		✓	✓
Juan Oso, John the Bear		✓	✓
La Estrella de Oro, The Gold Star		✓	✓
Animal Fables			
The Littlest Ant	✓	✓	
The Smelly Feet	✓	✓	
The Foolish Coyote	✓	✓	
Holiday Plays			
El Día de Los Muertos, The Fiesta of the Day of the Dead		✓	✓
La Aparicíon de Nuestra Señora de Guadalupe, The Miracle of Our Lady of Guadalupe		✓	✓
La Flor de La Noche Buena, The Flower of the Holy Night		✓	✓
Los Pastores, The Shepherds		✓	✓
An Historical Play			
La Batalla de Cinco de Mayo, The Battle of Cinco de Mayo		✓	✓

The plays also present a wide range of thematic choices. The simplest division of the plays corresponds to the two primary categories of traditional Hispanic plays, secular and religious holiday plays. The secular plays are the folktale and legend adaptations, the animal fables, and the historical play. The religious plays depict the events of several primary Hispanic holidays. Hispanic culture, like many other cultures of the world, is especially rich in celebrations centered around holiday traditions.

Casting

Most of the plays are written in a narrator format. The narrator format is particularly well suited for student plays because the narrated play is very similar in feeling and language to traditional storytelling. Because most of these plays are adaptations from the oral tradition, the storytelling format is especially appropriate.

An additional benefit of the narrated play format is that it provides an additional "good" part (the narrator), which can be cast either male or female. Or, the narrator part can be divided among several students, which adds even more roles to the production.

The narrator format gives students who are not dramatically inclined an important presence in the play's production. The narrator's part can easily be read instead of memorized, and this option provides less dramatically inclined students a successful way to participate.

Though several of the parts are clearly male or female parts, many of the parts can be cast either way. This flexibility of gender casting gives the director of the play great latitude. To its credit, educational theatre is especially free of the traditional casting constraints of professional theatre. Also, flexible casting decisions especially serve the educational goals of these plays.

One point of awareness is necessary, however, if the teacher or director does change the gender of a character. The teacher or student should read the play carefully and, where appropriate, change the gender references in the script to match the gender casting of the play.

Staging and Production

The primary staging suggestion is to follow the well-known dictum that "less is more." This production style reflects a philosophy of educational theatre that puts the young actor at the center of the theatrical experience. It also recognizes that the most valuable asset in a dramatic process with young performers is the student's imagination.

These plays are intended for nonprofessional production. By intent and design, they are short, easily produced scripts. A teacher could easily perform one of the scripts in a class period or select several of them to fill an assembly period.

The best dramatic strategy is to create the plays with an emphasis on dramatic characterization, emotional content, and secure performances. With a production choice of "less is more," the teacher-director is able to concentrate the resources of time and student energy into the most important area—the actor's performance. In this way, the emphasis of the play is where it belongs—on the student actor.

A well-established modern dramatic staging technique is the use of the unit-set. The unit-set is a singular, flexible space that is easily transformed by the use of dramatic imagination into the "place" in which dramatic action occurs. The unit-set practice is particularly appropriate for plays staged and produced in classrooms, cafeterias, gymnasiums, or recreational spaces.

With the addition of a few functional furniture pieces, the director can easily and inexpensively create and indicate places for dramatic action. The addition of a few carefully chosen hand props completes the necessary requirements for this style of theatre.

The plays in this book have simple staging requirements. Most elementary and junior high schools and classroom teachers do not have access to the resources or the training to mount productions with elaborate set and lighting effects. In recognition of this situation, the plays in this book have few staging needs or special effects requirements.

Often, a table and a few chairs are sufficient to indicate an interior space. Exterior spaces usually are best indicated by an empty space. The quick rearrangement of simple set pieces between scenes can indicate a change in time or location, if called for in the script.

Though a simple staging approach is recommended, many schools make it common practice to enlist volunteers to help in building and providing sets. Though this practice can definitely enhance a production, it is not a necessary requirement for a quality production. The best shows are those in which the actors are full of creative and focused energy, know their lines, are well rehearsed, are secure and relaxed on stage, and are having a lot of fun in the play. The emphasis in educational theatre with young performers is always on the actor and the performance.

Costumes

Consistent with the suggestions for staging and production, the following costume illustrations are meant to be an aid for creating a minimal but sufficient costume plot that fulfills several dramatic needs. First, the costumes are intended to indicate character and dramatic role. In this way, costumes help in creating the dramatic quality of "character distance," the ability for the audience to recognize the farmer from the mayor, the worker from the landowner, the peasant from the princess, and so on. Second, costumes are an aid in helping the imagination place the character in the proper time period and landscape. This is especially helpful in the minimal production style suggested in the staging section. Finally, it is important to recognize that costumes are one aspect of drama that students find most enjoyable. You can dispense with set pieces, but without costumes, students do not think that they are in a "real" play.

The following costume illustrations, figures 1–9, are grouped according to character type. Because many of the plays contain similar "types," a generic costume plot can serve several plays and dramatic situations. Also, the illustrations are guides to constructing character appearances with simple costume construction or inexpensive secondhand store purchases. The illustrations are also suggestions for cultural accuracy in costuming.

Spanish Language

The plays in this book contain a few Spanish-language words and phrases. Because these plays are not translated into Spanish, and because of the age level of the intended performers of the plays, the plays employ a minimal use of Spanish.

This use of the Spanish language gives the plays an enhanced Hispanic flavor and supports the plays' thematic content. The vocabulary used consists of simple, everyday words appropriate to a beginning conversational experience in Spanish. A glossary of Spanish words and phrases used is included to assist in the understanding and use of Spanish in the plays.

Peasant men: Simple shirts, pants (a little short is good), sandals or barefoot, and farmer hats. Eyebrow-pencil mustaches.
Old woman: A kerchief, long skirt, apron, shawl, and walking stick.
Robbers: Kerchiefs added to peasant man's costume.

Fig. 1. Peasant men, old woman, and robbers.

Peasant man: See figure 1.
Peasant woman: A simple, long skirt; apron; blouse; kerchief for hair; and sandals or barefoot.
Peasant child: Long, loose T-shirt; short pants; barefoot.

Fig. 2. Peasant man, woman, and child.

From ¡Teatro! Hispanic Plays for Young People. Copyright © 1996. Teacher Ideas Press. (800) 237-6124.

King and Queen: Long robes with embroidery or trim; crowns (optional: attach veils to the backs of the crowns).
Princesses: Variations on queen or señorita (see fig. 3).
Well-off woman: Like peasant woman but without apron or kerchief; with shoes, necklace, or brooch.
Well-off man: Like señores (see fig. 3) with the addition of a long cape.

Fig. 4. King and queen, princess, well-off man and woman.

Men: White shirts, with pleating if possible; black string ties; dark pants; socks; shoes; and broad-brimmed hats if possible.
Woman: Ruffled blouse, skirt, and shawl; flowers for hair; eyebrow-pencil "curls" on cheeks and beauty mark; red lips.

Fig. 3. Señores, Señorita—well-off men and a young woman.

From ¡Teatro! Hispanic Plays for Young People. Copyright © 1996. Teacher Ideas Press. (800) 237-6124.

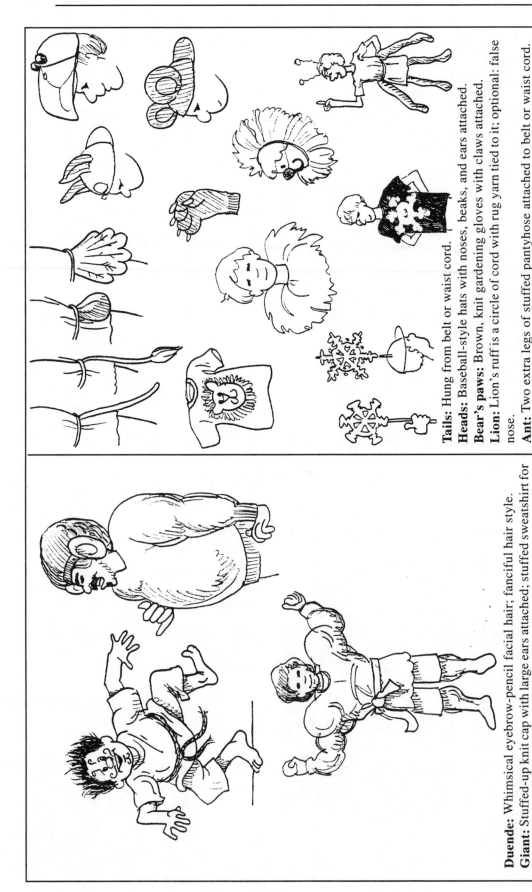

Tails: Hung from belt or waist cord.
Heads: Baseball-style hats with noses, beaks, and ears attached.
Bear's paws: Brown, knit gardening gloves with claws attached.
Lion: Lion's ruff is a circle of cord with rug yarn tied to it; optional: false nose.
Ant: Two extra legs of stuffed pantyhose attached to belt or waist cord.
T-shirt: With animal faces painted on front.
Snowflakes: Hand-held fiberboard.

Fig. 6. Animals and snowflakes.

Duende: Whimsical eyebrow-pencil facial hair; fanciful hair style.
Giant: Stuffed-up knit cap with large ears attached; stuffed sweatshirt for giant muscles.
Strong man: Stuffed muscles in arms, torso, and calves.

Fig. 5. Duende, giant, and strong man.

From *¡Teatro! Hispanic Plays for Young People.* Copyright © 1996. Teacher Ideas Press. (800) 237-6124.

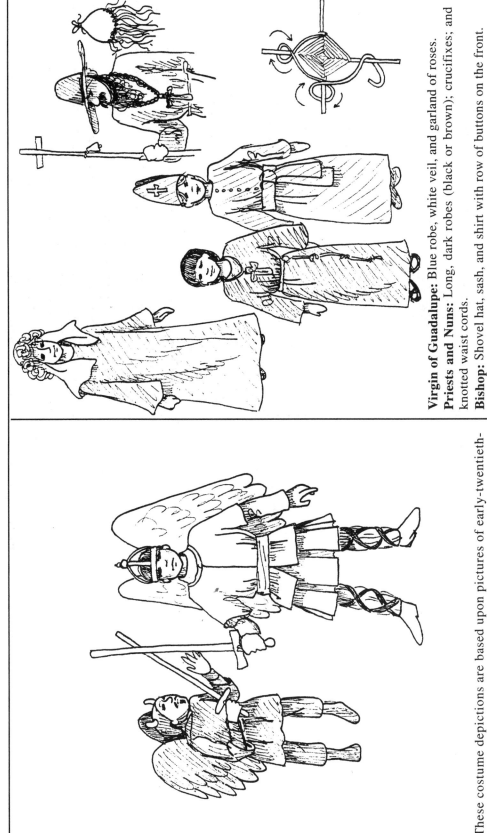

Virgin of Guadalupe: Blue robe, white veil, and garland of roses.
Priests and Nuns: Long, dark robes (black or brown); crucifixes; and knotted waist cords.
Bishop: Shovel hat, sash, and shirt with row of buttons on the front.
Hermit: Dressed like the priest, but slightly more disheveled, with a worn hat, beard (yarn knotted onto a cord), and a staff with a crosspiece on top and a small bell.
God's eye: Yarn wrapped around two sticks in a continuing series of loops.

Fig. 8. Religious characters, hermit, and God's eye.

These costume depictions are based upon pictures of early-twentieth-century village productions and are, historically, traditional costumes for these two characters. Similar costumes: dark for Lucifer, white for San Miguel. Lucifer has a horned cap and San Miguel has a crown. San Miguel has cross-gartered leggings.

Fig. 7. Lucifer and San Miguel.

From *¡Teatro! Hispanic Plays for Young People.* Copyright © 1996. Teacher Ideas Press. (800) 237-6124.

Military men: Uniforms with gold epaulets and braid, ribbon decorations, diagonal sashes, dark pants, and shoes. Tail coats can be made from ordinary dark shirts with the side seams split up and the fronts tucked into the pants. Epaulets can be made of small, gold, paper plates—cut "tassels" around the edges of the paper plates and fold them down.

Government officials: Dark suits with cutaway coats; white shirts with small, black bow ties; diagonal sashes. A satin stripe down the pants outseam would be appropriate.

Fig. 9. Military and government officials.

From ¡Teatro! Hispanic Plays for Young People. Copyright © 1996. Teacher Ideas Press. (800) 237-6124.

Part
I
Folktales

The Three Pieces of Good Advice

Introduction

The Three Pieces of Good Advice is one of the most common folktales in the Hispanic Southwest. It belongs to the category of stories known as Tales of Transformation, Magic, and Wisdom. Primarily, it is a tale about the gaining of wisdom through life's experiences.

Throughout the Southwest region, including Mexico, people tell various versions, with differences in the number of pieces of advice given, the reason the man leaves home, and whom the man finds embracing his wife at the end of the story. Of course, its consistent main quality is that of being a moral tale, for it contains the lessons of how to live the good and successful life. The version presented here is the most recognized in the Southwest.

Staging

The story takes place in a rural farming community. The staging is simple, with two exterior spaces, a farmyard and a forest road, and two interior spaces, a farmhouse and an inn. Each interior place can be indicated with chairs and a table. An exterior space is best indicated with an open stage.

Props

Three bags of money

A plate of food with a large *burrito* on it

A plate with a single *tortilla* on it

A ring of old keys

Costumes

See figures 1, 2, and 4 in the introduction to this book.

Cast of Characters

The Narrator

Juan, *a poor farmer, hardworking and honest*

Pablo, *Juan's friend, easygoing and carefree*

Enrique, *Juan's friend, lazy and afraid of work*

The Old Woman, *a wise, mysterious character*

Robber #1

Robber #2

Robber #3

Carlos, *the innkeeper, a loud, boisterous man*

Maria, *Carlos's wife, a quiet, timid woman*

Anna, *Juan's wife, proud and caring*

Manuel, *Juan's son, sincere and earnest*

Scene 1: In a farmyard.

The Narrator:	Once there was a poor farmer named Juan who struggled to make a living for his family. But no matter how hard he worked, things never seemed to work out. Finally, he decided to leave his village and go out into the world looking for work. Two of his *compadres*, or good friends, decided that they would go with him because they were having just as hard a time finding work as Juan was.

(*Juan and his friends Pablo and Enrique are standing around talking.*)

Pablo:	Juan, so what are you going to do? We heard that you were thinking of leaving and looking for work.
Enrique:	You haven't said a thing to us. I thought we were *compadres*.
Juan:	We are *compadres*. I just know you both. You'll slow me down, and you won't really want to work as hard or as much as I do.
Enrique:	Things have been just as hard for us. My family hasn't had a good meal in months. I can't remember when it's been so hard to make a simple living.
Juan:	Well, *compadres*, it's true. I was thinking about leaving and trying to find work out in the world. My *tio* went out and found good work right away. Every month he sends back one hundred dollars for his family.
Enrique:	One hundred dollars! What's he do?
Juan:	I don't know. He works! That's what I want to do.
Pablo:	Well, I'm going with you. If your *tio* can find work, so can I.
Enrique:	(*To Pablo.*) You'll never find work. You'll just slow us down. You're the laziest person I know. You're so lazy . . .
Pablo:	I'm not lazy. I can work in the field from sunrise to sunset. I can shoe horses twice as fast as you. I can fix tractors. I can—
Enrique:	You have to fix tractors. You're so lazy you never take care of them so they are always breaking down.
Pablo:	You just wait and see. I'll be the first one to find work. You'll see.
Juan:	This is just what I mean. You two will spend all of your time arguing about who can work the hardest; meanwhile I'll be the only one really looking for work.
Pablo:	Juan, wherever you go I'll be there working right by your side. You'll be lifting the heaviest box. So will I. Digging the deepest ditch. So will I. Sending the most money home. So will I. I'll be right there by your side.

From *¡Teatro! Hispanic Plays for Young People.* Copyright © 1996. Teacher Ideas Press. (800) 237-6124.

Enrique:	Me too. We're not *compadres* for nothing. And I know just the job I'm looking for. While you two are working outside, I'll have something inside. In the air-conditioning.
Pablo:	(*Looking off as if dreaming.*) Maybe I'll be with you, Enrique. No heavy lifting. Nothing dirty.
Enrique:	(*Joining the daydream.*) A secretary all for myself.
Pablo:	One hour for lunch.
Enrique:	One hundred dollars a week. No, two hundred.
Pablo:	Three hundred.
Enrique:	(*Overlapping with Pablo.*) Four hundred!
Pablo:	(*Overlapping with Enrique.*) Four hundred!
Juan:	(*Looking at his friends with disgust.*) I'm leaving bright and early in the morning. If you're not there, I'm leaving without you. You know the old *dicho* "The early bird gets the worm." (*He exits.*)
Pablo:	He thinks he's so much better than us.
Enrique:	(*Worried.*) Maybe he's right, though. Maybe it'll be a lot of work finding work.
Pablo:	How hard can it be. Even his *tio* found work.

(*Pablo and Enrique exit, laughing and talking about how easy it will be finding work and how easy the work will be.*)

Scene 2: On a forest road.

(*Juan, Pablo, and Enrique enter, traveling along a forest road.*)

The Narrator:	So the next morning, Juan and his two *compadres* set off looking for work. As in all stories, it wasn't long before they found the adventure they were looking for.
Pablo:	So, Juan. You haven't said much about what type of work you are looking for.
Juan:	There's not much to say. I said good-bye to my *familia*, asked for their blessing, and I will take what the good Lord sends to me.
Enrique:	How far did you say it was to the next village? And what did your wife pack for lunch? I'm already hungry.

From *¡Teatro! Hispanic Plays for Young People.* Copyright © 1996. Teacher Ideas Press. (800) 237-6124.

Pablo:	The village is over the mountains. I know a shortcut that can save us a couple of hours.
Juan:	I'm not so sure about that shortcut. Didn't the river flood and now the path is blocked?
Enrique:	You didn't answer my question. What did your wife pack for lunch?
Juan:	I didn't bring food for you. You were supposed to bring your own food.
Enrique:	(*Complaining.*) My own food! This was all your idea. You never told me we'd have to bring our own food or go over the mountain.
Pablo:	*Compadres*! Shhh! Somebody's coming. It could be the mountain bandits we heard about.
Enrique:	Great! Now we'll be robbed and left in the forest with nothing left!
Juan:	Both of you, just stop it. I knew I should have gone on this trip by myself. It's just an old woman walking down the same path as we are.

(*The Old Woman enters, carrying three bags of money.*)

Juan:	(*To the Old Woman.*) *Buenos días, señora.* Why are you traveling in the forest so early in the morning?
The Old Woman:	*Buenos días, señores.* I am just returning home from work. My work in the village is done, and it is time I return to my *familia*.
Pablo:	What's in the bags?
The Old Woman:	Just money. It is easier to carry it this way.
Enrique:	Just money! That is just what we are looking for. Where did you find it?
The Old Woman:	I didn't find it.
Juan:	*Señora.* Please tell us where there is a job that pays with such large bags of money. We are all looking for a job like that.
The Old Woman:	If it is work you are looking for, you will find work in the village over the mountain. But you must be willing to work very hard. In any job, you must earn your money with your hard work.
Enrique:	(*To Pablo.*) I was afraid she would say that.
Juan:	*Señora*, there are robbers in these forests. You must be more careful with your money.
The Old Woman:	(*Calmly.*) No one will harm me.

From *¡Teatro! Hispanic Plays for Young People*. Copyright © 1996. Teacher Ideas Press. (800) 237-6124.

Juan:	Please tell us where you got those bags of money. We are looking for work to make some money, and if there is some job paying with bags of money, we want to know about it.
The Old Woman:	Oh, if you want work, you'll find work. But I didn't get this money from some job. I got it by following good advice. In fact, I have a proposition for you. I will give each of you a bag of money, or I will give you three pieces of good advice.
Enrique:	Money or advice. What type of foolish choice is that, old woman? You've been out in the sun too long.
Pablo:	Maybe she's a *Duende* sent here to trick us.
Juan:	I don't think so. I think she's a wise old woman sent here to help us. We should listen more carefully to what she has to offer.
Enrique:	You can listen all you want but I want a bag of money. This is just the job I was looking for. A no-work-but-lots-of-money job!
Pablo:	Me too. Old woman, I'll take the bag of money.
Enrique:	Me too!
The Old Woman:	(*To Juan.*) And you?
Juan:	(*Hesitatingly.*) Well . . . I was raised to respect my elders, and one day a bag of money will run out and I'll be no better off than I am now. Maybe good advice will lead to more money in the long run . . . I'll take the advice.
Enrique:	Now you are as *loco* as the old woman! Will advice feed your children?
Juan:	I feel the old woman knows something we don't. Perhaps her advice will be good advice.
The Old Woman:	Are you sure?
Juan:	Yes, I want the advice!
The Old Woman:	Then come closer. (*Drawing Juan closer.*) Here is the advice. One. Keep to the main road, the well-traveled road. Do not go down strange roads, for they lead to danger. Two. Mind your own business. Keep quiet and only watch the affairs of others. Three. Think before you act. Don't do things without first looking carefully.
Enrique:	That's the advice! Am I glad I took the money.
Pablo:	Me too! (*To Juan.*) I'm sorry *compadre*, but now I am going back home. I really do hope you find work. (*Laughing.*) And remember, follow your good advice!

From *¡Teatro! Hispanic Plays for Young People.* Copyright © 1996. Teacher Ideas Press. (800) 237-6124.

Enrique:	(*Laughing with Pablo.*) Our poor *compadre*. Oh well, let's go home. We've worked long and hard enough for one day. (*Laughing again.*)
Pablo:	You know, I know a shortcut. We'll be home in time for supper.
Juan:	Remember the first piece of advice. You should take the main road. It's more traveled and it'll be safer.
Enrique:	We don't have to follow the old woman's advice. We took the bags of money, remember?

(*Pablo and Enrique both laugh.*)

Pablo:	What do you know? You know so little, you turn up your nose at money in favor of a few words from an old woman at the side of the road. We're going down the short path, and we'll be at home eating supper before you even get over the mountain path. Really, *compadre*, we wish you well, but *adiós*.

(*Pablo and Enrique exit, laughing and carrying their bags of money. The Old Woman exits, carrying the remaining bag of money. Juan exits, dejectedly.*)

Scene 3: On another forest road.

(*Pablo and Enrique enter, traveling along a less-traveled forest road.*)

The Narrator:	So Juan's two friends made their choice. But soon they found out it is sometimes better to follow good advice.
Pablo:	You know, I feel bad for Juan. But he made his own decision. How much money do you think is in the bags?
Enrique:	A lot! I can't wait to get home to count it. I'm really glad we took this shortcut. Soon we'll be home. Food, *familia*, money. Things couldn't be better.
Pablo:	Are you sure this is the right way?
Enrique:	Of course I'm sure.

(*Suddenly, the three Robbers enter, ambushing Pablo and Enrique. The Robbers have their faces covered with bandannas.*)

Robber #1:	This must be our lucky day. Two fools walking through our part of the forest.
Robber #2:	Carrying bags of . . . (*Sarcastically.*) . . . now what could be in those bags?
Robber #3:	Money? Nahhh. That would be too easy.
Robber #1:	Like taking candy from a baby.

From *¡Teatro! Hispanic Plays for Young People.* Copyright © 1996. Teacher Ideas Press. (800) 237-6124.

Robber #2:	Or money from *locos*.
Robber #1:	(*Very graciously.*) *Buenos días, señores.* What brings you to our part of the forest?
Robber #2:	Perhaps you are lost. Like little sheep who have lost their way.
Robber #3:	Could we help you with those bags? They look sooooo heavy.
Enrique:	(*Very frightened.*) Oh no. We're not lost. We were just taking a shortcut home. If fact, we better just keep right on our way.

(*Enrique tries to walk around the Robbers, but they block his way.*)

Robber #3:	Don't be in such a hurry. It's not friendly.
Robber #2:	(*In a threatening voice.*) We wouldn't want to be unfriendly, would we?
Pablo:	(*Shaking with fear.*) No . . . no . . . We're very friendly.
Robber #1:	Let me help you with these bags.
Enrique:	Oh, we don't need any help. There's nothing in these bags.
Pablo:	(*Looking at Enrique and shaking his head to say no.*) Yeah, nothing.
Enrique:	Especially not money.

(*Pablo jabs Enrique.*)

Robber #1:	(*Grabbing the bags of money.*) Give us the bags! (*To the other robbers.*) Tie them up!
Enrique:	Help!
Pablo and Enrique:	Help!

(*As Pablo and Enrique yell for help, the Robbers tie them up and exit with the bags of money*).

Pablo:	See, I told you this was the wrong path.
Enrique:	No, I told you. We should have followed that good advice.

(*Pablo and Enrique hop off-stage*).

Scene 4: Inside an inn.

(*Juan and Carlos enter. Carlos gets busy cleaning a table.*)

The Narrator:	Meanwhile, Juan had finally walked over the mountain, taking the main, well-traveled road, of course, and had come to an inn where he hoped to find a place to rest and maybe even some work.

From *¡Teatro! Hispanic Plays for Young People*. Copyright © 1996. Teacher Ideas Press. (800) 237-6124.

Juan: | (*Approaching Carlos.*) Excuse me *señor*, I just walked over the mountain and I'm really tired. I am looking for a place to rest, and tomorrow I will begin to look for work in your village. Do you know of any place needing a good worker?

Carlos: | (*In a loud, brusque voice.*) Looking for work, eh? Well you came to the right place. My business keeps growing, and I need another worker to help in the kitchen. Can you cook?

Juan: | *Sí señor. Tamales, frijoles, tortillas.* You name it, I can cook it.

Carlos: | But are you a good cook? Anyone can cook, but not everyone can make it taste good.

Juan: | Let me earn my job. I will cook dinner for you tonight, and if it is any good, then give me the job.

Carlos: | That's the best deal I've heard yet. If it works out, I get not only a good worker, but a good meal, too. And if you're no good, it's better I find out before I give you the job.

The Narrator: | Juan cooked as he had never cooked before. He had often cooked for his *familia*, and they all liked his food, so he was confident that he would get the job. But he was still nervous as he watched and waited for the innkeeper to finish his food.

(*Juan puts a plate of food before Carlos. The plate is filled with a large* burrito. *Juan paces and watches nervously as Carlos eats the* burrito).

Carlos: | (*Wiping his mouth after finishing his meal.*) That was delicious. You have the job. You can stay in one of the rooms upstairs and begin cooking tomorrow. That was delicious! Now that you are cooking such good meals, I'm going to have to raise the prices.

(*Juan and Carlos exit.*)

Scene 5: Inside the inn.

The Narrator: | Juan soon settled into his job. He enjoyed it and was happy to be working. Often he thought about his two *compadres* and wondered what had happened to them after they had returned home. He still didn't see any use for the advice the old woman had given him, but he hoped that one day it might come in handy. Every month he would send money home to his *familia*, and he hoped that one day he would have enough money saved to send for them. After he had worked at the inn for several months, he began to notice something very strange.

From *¡Teatro! Hispanic Plays for Young People.* Copyright © 1996. Teacher Ideas Press. (800) 237-6124.

(*Carlos and Maria enter, carrying two plates of food. On one plate is a large* burrito. *On the other plate is only one plain* tortilla. *They sit down and begin to eat. Carlos eats from the plate with the large* burrito *while Maria only nibbles from the* tortilla.)

Carlos: | This is delicious! That new cook is wonderful, isn't he?

Maria: | (*In a quiet voice.*) Yes, dear.

Carlos: | Juan, come here.

(*Juan enters, hurrying.*)

Juan: | Yes, you called. Is everything okay?

Carlos: | Couldn't be better. Bring me another *burrito*, and this time smother it with more green chile.

Juan: | (*To Maria.*) *Señora*, could I bring you something more?

Maria: | Oh no, this is fine.

Juan: | (*To the audience.*) You know, I've worked here for several months now and I've never seen the innkeeper's wife eat anything more than a *tortilla*. I wonder if anything is wrong with her. Maybe she is sick. I know a *curandera* who can usually cure anything. Maybe I could offer my services . . . but maybe I better not. I remember the second bit of advice the old woman gave me—mind my own business. Maybe this is a good time to use some of that good advice. I haven't seen any use for it yet, but I gave up a bag of money for it, so I might as well use some of it. I'll just mind my own business. (*To Maria.*) Well, if you need anything, just let me know.

Maria: | I will

Carlos: | (*He has been watching Juan carefully.*) This is delicious!

(*All exit.*)

Scene 6: Inside the inn.

(*Juan enters, and begins working, setting the table and wiping the glasses.*)

The Narrator: | The months turned into years, and through the years Juan missed his family greatly and dreamed of the day he could bring them to live with him. He was always curious as to why the innkeeper's wife only ate *tortillas*, but he was determined to use at least one piece of advice the old woman had given him. He just figured that some things in life you'll never know about. One day the innkeeper and his wife approached Juan as he was working.

From ¡*Teatro! Hispanic Plays for Young People.* Copyright © 1996. Teacher Ideas Press. (800) 237-6124.

(Carlos and Maria enter, and approach Juan.)

Carlos:	Juan, I need to talk to you.
Juan:	Is anything wrong? I've been doing my best. Is something wrong with the food?
Maria:	No, Juan. Nothing is wrong. In fact, things couldn't be better. Sit down, our friend.
Juan:	But I have my cooking to do.
Carlos:	Sit down. Soon someone else will be doing the cooking.
Juan:	*(Very worried.)* Please *señor*, don't fire me. I've been doing my best and my *familia* depends upon me to send money home. Just tell me what to do and I'll fix it.
Carlos:	I'm not going to fire you. You've been a great worker. So great that I have a special gift for you. I am an old man now, and my wife and I are ready to retire. As you know, we have never been fortunate enough to have any children, so there is no one for me to leave this business to.
Maria:	Over the years, it has grown into a successful business, even more so since you started cooking for us. And it would not be right to close it down just because we are retiring.
Carlos:	We are rich now, and we want to give you this inn for your own business.
Juan:	*(Stammering with disbelief.)* But . . . but . . . why me?
Maria:	Because you minded your own business.
Carlos:	Years ago, we decided that we would leave our inn to the person who could mind his own business. As you have seen, my wife eats very little. There is a reason for that, but it is a reason we wish to keep to ourselves. In the past, people have asked us about it and we have always felt is was our own business. So we decided that whoever minded his own business would get the business. You are that man.
Juan:	*(Overcome with joy.)* Thank you, thank you so very much. I will work so hard to keep the inn the wonderful place you have made it.
Carlos:	We know you will. That's why we are giving it to you. You've become like a son to us.
Juan:	Now I can have my *familia* come and join me here and share in all the good fortune that has come my way.
Carlos:	But tell us one thing. What made you a man who minds his own business?

From *¡Teatro! Hispanic Plays for Young People*. Copyright © 1996. Teacher Ideas Press. (800) 237-6124.

Juan:	Let's just say that in my life I've been given some good advice.
Maria:	Everyone is given good advice every now and then. But you listened to it and followed it. Here are the keys to the inn. It's yours now . . . innkeeper. (*Juan, Carlos, and Maria hug and exit.*)

Scene 7: At Juan's farmhouse.

The Narrator:	Juan was overjoyed. Now he knew that he was right to follow the advice of the old woman, for now he could have his family come and live with him, and he could take care of them the way he had always wanted to. As soon as he got the inn running smoothly under his ownership, he rushed back to his home to tell his family the good news. But as he came to his farmhouse, he was startled by what he saw.

(*Juan, Anna, and Manuel enter. On one side of the stage, Juan acts his scene. On the other side of the stage, Anna and Manuel sit and talk.*)

Juan:	(*To the audience.*) Finally, I am back home. Everything looks just as it did when I left so many years ago to find work. I will surprise my family with my return and even more with the story of my good fortune.

(*Juan mimes the following action as the narrator speaks.*)

The Narrator:	Juan crept up to one of the windows and looked in. He was shocked to see his wife embracing another man. He was about to burst into his house and confront the two when he suddenly remembered the third piece of advice.
Juan:	(*To the audience.*) The third piece of advice. Think before you act. The second piece of advice about minding my own business served me well, so perhaps it is best if I follow another piece of advice. I will knock on the door first, and then enter the house. Perhaps there is a good explanation for the troubling sight I have just seen.

(*Juan mimes knocking on the door.*)

Anna:	Just a moment . . . (*She talks to Manuel. As she is talking, Juan enters the room and overhears their conversation.*) You must go now. You have my blessing for your journey. I will miss you here at the farm, but it is time for you to seek your fortune in the world. If only your father could see you. He would be so proud of his son. All grown up and ready to go into the world.
Manuel:	All these years I have carried the memory of my father in my heart. The first thing I am going to do is journey over the mountain and find my father and join him in the work he does. One day, we will send for you and the rest of the family and we will be reunited as a family once again. I promise this to you, mother dearest.

From *¡Teatro! Hispanic Plays for Young People.* Copyright © 1996. Teacher Ideas Press. (800) 237-6124.

Juan: | (*Entering the room.*) Manuel, your father has returned. My greatest wishes have come true. I have been gone so long that looking in the window I didn't recognize my son, but now I see that you are my own son grown up.

(*Anna, Manuel, and Juan embrace.*)

Juan: | Sit down, both of you. I have the most amazing story to tell you about three pieces of good advice.

From *¡Teatro! Hispanic Plays for Young People.* Copyright © 1996. Teacher Ideas Press. (800) 237-6124.

The Most Interesting Gift of All

Introduction

The Most Interesting Gift of All is a wonderful tale from the category of stories known as Tales of Transformation, Magic, and Wisdom. Its playful atmosphere is enhanced by the magical objects that are at the center of the story.

Traditional stories abound with instances in which characters encounter objects with magical capabilities. Snow White's "Mirror, Mirror, on the wall," Jack's magical beans, and Cinderella's pumpkin and mice are several examples of traditional storytelling's use of transformational objects as a central story element.

Staging

The staging can be simply accomplished with the use of chairs and tables. The interior scenes are indicated with arranged chairs to represent a formal main room.

Props

A magician's bag

A crystal ball

Polishing rags

A sword

Juggling balls

An old magician's cart

An old woman's bag

An old mirror

A bottle with leaves in it

Mixing bowls

A mixing table

Herbs

Costumes

See figures 1 and 3 in the introduction to this book.

Cast of Characters

The Narrator

The Ornales Brothers:

  Santiago, *the oldest*

  Estevan, *the middle*

  Frankie, *the youngest*

La Coqueta, *a young, flirtatious girl*

Don Roberto, *the father of La Coqueta*

The Magician, *a gregarious and flamboyant circus performer*

The Old Woman, *from the woods, mysterious and wise*

The Curandera, *wise in the old ways, a woman who knows the magical healing arts*

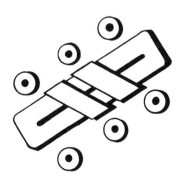

Scene 1: The Ornales house.

(*As the narrator speaks, the three Ornales Brothers walk on the stage and pose. As the narrator speaks, he/she goes to each brother and indicates who he is.*)

The Narrator: Once there were three brothers, the three Ornales brothers. The eldest was Santiago Ornales. He was the leader of the family. Proud and measured in his ways. The second brother was Estevan Ornales. He was quiet and sincere in his manner. The youngest brother was Frankie Ornales. Frankie was the most playful of the three brothers. Young and still growing, he was full of the confidant manners of youth. The three Ornales brothers had one problem, however. They all loved the same woman, La Coqueta, a young, beautiful woman who lived in the city. The youngest brother had given her the name La Coqueta because she was such a flirt whenever she was around them. One day the three brothers decided it was time to declare their intentions to La Coqueta.

Santiago: Today, my brothers, you will learn why women prefer the older, more mature man. I intend to ask for the hand of La Coqueta in marriage. I do not hold it against you that you love the same woman as me, but after she has chosen, you must give up your feelings for her because she will be mine.

Estevan: (*Laughing to himself, then gaining control.*) Oh brother, I give you my respect as my older brother, but I do not see La Coqueta saying yes to you. She is kind to you out of respect for your age, but I have seen her looking at me whenever she has the chance. Brother, I am afraid you are going to make a fool out of yourself today. But I agree with you on one thing. After today, you must give up your feelings for her if we are to remain brothers.

Frankie: You two sound like a couple of *viejitos* who don't know that their time for young women is over. La Coqueta is young and fun-loving. Even if she doesn't choose me, she would never choose someone as old as either of you. You both are wise from experience, but that is not what La Coqueta wants in her husband. Her uncle or father, yes. But not her husband. You will see. I am the only one with a real chance for the hand of La Coqueta.

(*All exit, laughing and teasing one another.*)

Scene 2: The house of La Coqueta.

(*Don Roberto enters.*)

Narrator It is a Hispanic tradition that the man must ask permission of the woman's parents before asking the woman for her hand in marriage. So the three Ornales brothers all went to speak with La Coqueta's father, Don Roberto.

From *¡Teatro! Hispanic Plays for Young People*. Copyright © 1996. Teacher Ideas Press. (800) 237-6124.

Don Roberto:	(*Pacing and nervous.*) Oh, here come the three Ornales brothers. I don't know what to do. I have never even heard of three brothers all asking for the hand of the same woman before. And why my daughter? She is still so young, much too young to be married! She is still a child. Why, the nerve of these three men. I will refuse to allow them to ask for her hand in marriage . . . But then they are the Ornales brothers. Their ranch is one of the largest in the valley. And they are men of honor. My daughter will be well cared for. And I do have my own old age to think of . . . Yes, I have decided. Any of the Ornales brothers would make a fine husband for my daughter. But what if my daughter refuses all three of them? Then we will have lost the chance of a lifetime. Oh, it was so much easier in the old days when daughters had no say in these matters. Oh, here they are.

(*The three Ornales Brothers enter.*)

Santiago:	*Buenos días*, Don Roberto. How is your health?
Don Roberto:	Fine, thank you. And how are you and your brothers?
Santiago:	We are doing well, thank you.
Don Roberto:	And your mother and father?
Estevan:	Their health is fine.
Frankie:	(*Aside to Santiago.*) Santiago, why so much small talk? Let's get down to business.
Santiago:	Patience. We must first pay our respects to Don Roberto. This is exactly why La Coqueta will never choose you.
Estevan:	Don Roberto, I am sure that you have guessed the purpose of my and my brothers' visit. We have come to ask for the hand of your daughter in marriage.
Santiago:	We realize that it is highly unusual for three brothers to all ask for the hand of the same woman, but we all love her and have agreed among ourselves that it is only proper for you and your daughter to choose from among us.
Don Roberto:	Oh good *señores*, I wish it were as simple as that. I know that you all are men of integrity and means, and that any one of you would make a good husband for my daughter. But these are new times, and while I give you permission to ask for my daughter's hand. I cannot say what her answer will be. My daughter is a very headstrong woman, and she might say no to all three of you!
Santiago:	Thank you, Don Roberto. (*Bowing deeply.*) We are honored by the privilege of asking for your daughter's hand.
Frankie:	Oh brother! It's talk like this that is exactly why she will never say yes to you.

From *¡Teatro! Hispanic Plays for Young People*. Copyright © 1996. Teacher Ideas Press. (800) 237-6124.

Don Roberto:	She is waiting in the parlor. She has requested that she meet with each one of you alone so she can get the true measure of each of you without being in competition with the others.

(*All exit.*)

Scene 3: The parlor room.

(*On one side of the stage sits La Coqueta. On the other side pace the three Ornales Brothers, each waiting his turn to speak with La Coqueta.*)

Santiago:	(*Clears his throat and nervously approaches La Coqueta.*) Good afternoon La, oops, I mean *Señorita*. I have come to ask for your hand in marriage. Please know that I love you, and that all that I have, which is considerable, being the oldest son of my family, will be yours. I know that I am older than my brothers, but I am finished with my wild days, and I will make you a good and trustworthy husband.
La Coqueta:	I am honored by your request. But I have promised to hear the requests of your two brothers also. Please give me the time to hear their requests, and then I shall give you my decision.
Santiago:	Yes, of course, *Señorita*. I await your answer. Please give my words your deepest consideration. (*He bows deeply and joins his brothers at the side of the stage.*)
Santiago:	She is so beautiful! I can't believe what I did.
Frankie:	What happened? What did she say?
Santiago:	I almost called her La Coqueta!

(*All laugh.*)

Estevan:	No way!
Santiago:	Yes. I was so nervous I could barely talk.
Estevan:	Well, now it is time for her to hear from a real man. (*He approaches La Coqueta. He, too, is nervous and clears his throat before speaking.*) Good afternoon La . . . I mean *Señorita*. I also have come to ask for your hand in marriage. What I have to offer is all my love and the promise that I will honor and take care of you for all of my life. If you choose me as your husband, you will make me the happiest man in the world. Know that I will always make sure that your family is cared for and that as long as I am alive they will be welcome at my house. I will dedicate my life to making you happy.

From *¡Teatro! Hispanic Plays for Young People.* Copyright © 1996. Teacher Ideas Press. (800) 237-6124.

La Coqueta:	I am pleased with your words, and I know they come from your heart. I am honored by your request. But I have promised to hear the requests of your two brothers also. Please give me the time to consider their requests, and then I shall give you my decision.
Estevan:	Thank you for your kind words. I wait for you decision, and please give me your deepest consideration. (*He bows deeply and joins his brothers at the side of the stage.*)
Santiago:	So what happened?
Estevan:	I can't believe I did the same thing you did. It was so hot in there I thought I was going to faint. I almost called her La Coqueta, too.

(*All laugh.*)

Frankie:	You both are a disgrace to the Ornales family name. It is up to me, the youngest, to bring honor back to the family. After you two, she will easily say yes to me.
Estevan:	Well good luck. It's not as easy as you think.
Frankie:	Make way for the real man of the family. (*He approaches La Coqueta. He, too, is very nervous.*) Good afternoon La . . . oh I mean, uh, *Señorita.* Thank you for giving me the honor of asking for your hand in marriage. I know that, as the youngest brother, I do not have as much to offer you as my brothers. But know that I am a hard worker and that someday I will have as much as my brothers have and that you will never want for anything. Because I am the youngest, we will have our full lives together. We will be able to enjoy our youth and grow into old age together. I have never been with any woman, and if you accept my offer of marriage, I will never be with any woman but you.
La Coqueta:	Your words would move any woman's heart. But know that I must give my full consideration to your two brothers also. Please wait outside, and soon I will have an answer for all three of you.
Frankie:	We all will wait for your answer. And please give my words their fair consideration. They do come from my deepest heart.
La Coqueta:	Wait outside with your brothers and I'll be there soon with my answer.

(*Frankie joins his brothers at the side of the stage to compare stories.*)

Santiago:	Brothers, there is nothing to do but wait.
Estevan:	Shhh! Here they come.
Frankie:	I hope she chose me.

(*The Ornales Brothers are joined by La Coqueta and Don Roberto.*)

From *¡Teatro! Hispanic Plays for Young People.* Copyright © 1996. Teacher Ideas Press. (800) 237-6124.

Don Roberto:	*Señores*, my daughter has asked to speak to you.
La Coqueta:	I am very honored and flattered that three such fine men would want my hand in marriage. To tell the truth, it is too hard for me to make up my mind. I need a little more time to think about it. Meanwhile, I give you a challenge to help me decide. Come back in a week, and whoever brings me the most interesting gift will greatly help his case with me.

(Don Roberto looks at the three brothers and shrugs his shoulders as if to say, "I told you so." Then La Coqueta and Don Roberto exit. Each of the three Ornales Brothers, in turn, addresses the audience.)

Santiago:	*(To the audience.)* I once traveled with a circus and I knew a magician, an old friend of mine, who could do the most wonderful tricks. He could make balls multiply, scarves disappear, rings link together and come apart in unseen ways. Once I even saw him cut a woman in half. Surely he would have something for me that would be the most interesting gift in the world. *(He exits.)*
Estevan:	*(To the audience.)* I know where an old woman lives in the forest. People tell stories about her magic powers. Late at night, they tell stories of the magic they see and hear coming from her house. Perhaps she would be willing to give me one of her magic objects. Even one small object would be the most interesting gift in all the world. *(He exits.)*
Frankie:	*(To the audience.)* I know a *curandera*, a healer, who knows how to cure even the sickest person. She has some plants and herbs with powerful magic. She will be able to give me something to win the hand of La Coqueta. *(He exits.)*

Scene 4: At a circus, outside a magician's tent. An old cart sits nearby.

(The Magician is busy polishing his crystal ball.)

Narrator	The eldest brother traveled for days until he found the campsite of the circus. He looked throughout the circus camp until he saw the familiar wagon of his old friend The Magician. He said a silent prayer to himself that the magician would have the winning gift for him.

(Santiago enters.)

Santiago:	Good friend, remember me? It is your old friend, Santiago.
The Magician:	Of course I remember you. How could I ever forget the times we shared when you traveled with the circus.
Santiago:	It's been a long time.

From *¡Teatro! Hispanic Plays for Young People.* Copyright © 1996. Teacher Ideas Press. (800) 237-6124.

The Magician:	Not in circus time. In the circus, time stands still. It's all part of the magic. Remember, once you are in the circus, the circus is in you forever. So my friend, are you coming back to the circus?
Santiago:	Not really. I have come looking for a favor. You know that I have done you many favors, and now it is time for me to ask one of you.
The Magician:	For you, anything!
Santiago:	Well, it can't be just anything.
The Magician:	A new trick. (*With a flourish, the Magician brings each object out of his magician's bag.*) Swords that disappear. Balls that glow in the dark . . .
Santiago:	No, something even more special than your usual tricks.
The Magician:	Are you in trouble?
Santiago:	Only in my heart. I am in love with a beautiful woman and I have asked for her hand in marriage. To win her hand, I need the most interesting gift in the world.
The Magician:	(*Suddenly very secretive and looking around to make sure no one is hearing him.*) I have just the thing! I have never used it in the act because I didn't want anyone to know I had it. Once on a journey in another part of the world I met a dying magician. He gave me this gift with a promise that I would use it well. I can't think of a better use for it than to help my old friend win the heart of his loved one. Do you see my old cart here?
Santiago:	That old cart! Don't try to play a joke on me now. This is really important to me.
The Magician:	(*Excitedly.*) I know it doesn't look like much, but that's the secret of it! It can fly and take you anywhere in the world you want to go. But don't let anyone see you use it or they'll know your secret.
Santiago:	Thank you, dear friend. This is just the gift to win the hand of La Coqueta.
Magician:	La who?
Santiago:	No time to explain now. I have to hurry. (*He exits pulling the cart.*)

(*The Magician exits.*)

Scene 5: Deep in the forest.

(*Estevan enters, walking in circles, apparently lost.*)

Narrator	The middle brother traveled deep into a nearby forest. Soon he was lost and he began to wonder if he would ever find the old woman's house.

From *¡Teatro! Hispanic Plays for Young People.* Copyright © 1996. Teacher Ideas Press. (800) 237-6124.

Estevan:	I know it is around here somewhere. Let's see. Follow the path until you come to a clearing. Did that. Then follow the river. Did that. Look for the giant tree with the red markings. But which giant tree with the red markings. There are hundreds of them.

(Suddenly the Old Woman enters, as if appearing out of nowhere.)

The Old Woman:	Looking for something, my dear young man?
Estevan:	Whoa! Where did you come from. I was just here and you weren't anywhere.
The Old Woman:	Oh, I've been around, but you weren't looking hard enough.
Estevan:	Well, I was actually looking for the old woman who lives in these woods. But I couldn't find her house.
The Old Woman:	Maybe she doesn't live in a house.
Estevan:	Doesn't live in a house? No, I really think she lives in a house. Please help me. I have to find her.
The Old Woman:	Don't be in such a hurry. Maybe she found you.
Estevan:	*(Becoming scared.)* You . . . you . . .
The Old Woman:	Maybe. What brings you deep into these woods? What is it you want from a little old woman in the woods? There is not much I can give you. As you see, I have very little.
Estevan:	*(To himself.)* Oh no. This isn't the old woman I was looking for. She is as lost as I am.
The Old Woman:	*(As if reading his mind.)* It's true that you are lost. But I'm not lost at all.
Estevan:	*(To himself again.)* She read my mind. Maybe she is the woman I'm looking for! *(Now talking to the old woman.)* Señora, I have asked a woman for her hand in marriage. She has challenged me to find the most interesting gift in the world before she accepts my offer. Is there any way you can help me? There is nothing I can give you in return, but I promise that one day I will pay you back.
The Old Woman:	Perhaps I can help you. I do have a few special things. And don't worry about paying me back. In cases like this one, I usually get what I want sooner or later. *(Looking into her bag.)* Now let's see. Oh, here is just the thing for a young lady. *(She pulls out an old beat-up mirror.)* Just the thing!
Estevan:	*(In a dejected voice.)* That's all? An old mirror.
The Old Woman:	An old mirror to you, young man. But to the owner of the mirror, it is a special mirror. Whenever you look into it, you will see whatever you want to see.

From ¡*Teatro! Hispanic Plays for Young People*. Copyright © 1996. Teacher Ideas Press. (800) 237-6124.

(*Estevan tries to look into the mirror, but the old woman pulls it away before he can look into it.*)

The Old Woman:	Not yet. You must be careful with the mirror, because if you drop it, and it breaks, the person you are looking at will die. (*She hands the mirror to Estevan.*)
Estevan:	Thank you. Thank you very much. I'll pay you back some day. I promise.

(*As Estevan is looking into the mirror, he doesn't notice the Old Woman exit.*)

Estevan:	Now where did she go? (*He exits.*)

Scene 6: At the curandera's house.

(*The Curandera is busy mixing herbs together on a table.*)

Narrator	The youngest brother immediately went to the house of the *curandera*. He hoped and prayed that his idea was a good one and that soon he would be able to give La Coqueta the most interesting gift of all.

(*Frankie enters.*)

Frankie:	(*Calling out.*) Curandera. Curandera.
The Curandera:	Yes, yes. Don't yell so loud. You'll wake the dead.
Frankie:	*Curandera*, once you helped my mother when my father was very ill. She told me you have special herbs and plants, very special healing herbs and plants.
The Curandera:	Who is ill? Maybe I can be of some help.
Frankie:	No one is ill. I have asked a beautiful young woman for her hand in marriage. Would you please help me win her hand? I need to find the most interesting gift in the world.
The Curandera:	You have come to the right place. I have just the thing to turn a young woman's fancy in your favor. (*She reaches into a bag she is carrying and gives him a bottle.*) Here. Just one of these leaves ground up will bring the dead back to life. Take them and use them carefully. If people see you use them, they will think you have my special knowledge and they will never leave you alone. Remember, you do not have the power. I am just giving you a few leaves.
Frankie:	A few leaves will be just enough. Thank you, *curandera*. I thank you. My mother thanks you. My father thanks you. Everyone thanks you!

(*Frankie and the Curandera exit.*)

From *¡Teatro! Hispanic Plays for Young People.* Copyright © 1996. Teacher Ideas Press. (800) 237-6124.

Scene 7: On a path in the forest.

The Narrator:	Now each of the three Ornales brothers had what he thought was the most interesting gift in the world. It just so happened that, hurrying back to the house of La Coqueta, they met each other on the road back to the city.

(The three Ornales Brothers enter. Estevan and Frankie are carrying their gifts. Santiago is empty-handed.)

Santiago:	Estevan, Frankie! What luck to meet you here. Have you been successful in your search for the gift to impress La Coqueta?
Estevan:	Have I! Look what I got from the old . . . wait a minute, why should I show you my magic gift? Where is yours?
Santiago:	Estevan, don't be like that. It is up to La Coqueta to decide which is the best gift. Remember that we were brothers before La Coqueta even came along and we will be brothers still even after she chooses my gift as the best one.
Frankie:	Maybe not, brother. Mine is a very good gift.
Estevan:	Mine too. Look. It's a mirror. (*He hold up the mirror to show to his brothers.*)
Frankie:	That old mirror? Now I know she's mine.
Estevan:	Not so fast, brother. Look into the mirror and think of our beautiful La Coqueta.

(All three brothers crowd around the mirror and look into it.)

Santiago:	It's a magic mirror, isn't it?
Estevan:	Yes. It will show whatever we are thinking of.
Frankie:	Look! There is Don Roberto and his wife . . . but why are they dressed in black and why are they crying?!
Santiago:	Look! There is our beloved La Coqueta. She is in the bed and the priest is giving her the last sacraments. Brothers, while we have been gone, something terrible has happened to La Coqueta. We must return at once.
Estevan:	We will never get there in time. It is too far away.
Santiago:	Quick, my cart is just under the tree. Hurry and get into it. I'll tell you on the way. We'll be there in no time at all.
Frankie:	In the cart?
Santiago:	Don't ask questions. Just get in!

(All exit.)

From *¡Teatro! Hispanic Plays for Young People.* Copyright © 1996. Teacher Ideas Press. (800) 237-6124.

Scene 8: At the home of La Coqueta.

The Narrator:	With the magical powers of the cart, the brothers quickly returned to the home of La Coqueta. Immediately, they rushed to see La Coqueta and found out that she had suddenly fallen very ill and was in danger of dying. The youngest brother was able to bring her back to life with the special leaves the *curandera* had given him.

(Don Roberto, La Coqueta, and the three Ornales Brothers enter.)

Don Roberto:	*Señores*, you have my deepest gratitude for saving the life of my daughter. I still do not understand however how you were able to do it so quickly.
Estevan:	I used my gift of the magic mirror to discover that she had fallen gravely ill.
Santiago:	I used my gift of a magic flying cart to transport us here as quickly as possible.
Frankie:	And I used my gift of the special leaves from the *curandera* to take the sickness away from her.
Don Roberto:	I am forever in your debt.
Santiago:	And now La . . . oops, I mean *Señorita*. You have seen our gifts. Which one of them is the most interesting gift in the world?
La Coqueta:	I wish to thank each of you for sharing with me the wonderful gifts you have brought back. Especially because you used them to save my life. But to tell the truth, this has only made it harder for me to choose. Each gift was as wonderful and powerful as the other. Now we must do something else to help me make up my mind. Go out into the field and each of you shoot an arrow into the sky. Whoever shoots the arrow the farthest will help his cause in asking for my hand in marriage.

(The Ornales Brothers groan "Oh no!" as Don Roberto shrugs his shoulders. All exit.)

Scene 9: In a field.

(As the Narrator speaks, the three Ornales Brothers mime the action of shooting an arrow into the sky. After the arrows are shot, all the characters mime looking at the arrows as they fly away.)

The Narrator:	The three brothers went out into the field with their strongest bows and their lightest arrows. With all their might they drew back the bowstrings and sent three arrows flying as far as they could . . . And now this story comes to an end. To this day the arrows have not come down yet, and the three Ornales brothers are still waiting to see who would win the hand of La Coqueta.

From *¡Teatro! Hispanic Plays for Young People*. Copyright © 1996. Teacher Ideas Press. (800) 237-6124.

Blanca Flor

White Flower

Introduction

Blanca Flor translates into "white flower." This traditional story, a transformation and magic story, is known under several other titles. In some areas, it is known as *Paloma Blanca,* "white dove," while in others the young woman is called Jujuyana. Whatever the title, the story remains similar in its dramatic aspects. All the versions involve the flight of a young woman and her rescuer from the dangers of a threatening situation.

The dramatic events of her "throwing" personal belongings and their transformation into natural objects is one of the most common elements in this type of story. Traditionally, the objects are a comb, a brush, and a mirror. Traditionally, the objects become, respectively, a fence, a forest, and a lake. In this version of the story, the objects transform into different objects, which marks this version with its identifiable Hispanic characteristics. Traditional European tales such as this one all have this common magical transformation of objects at the escape phase of the story.

The ending of this story is a variation on a common theme found in all stories of this type—the reuniting of young lovers through magic and transformation.

Staging

Because of the many dramatic moments of magic and transformation in this story, the play uses the dramatic device of the narrator more than most stories. In the many instances in which the narrator is describing action and events, the actors in the play act out through mime action the events being described by the narrator.

The actors should strive through miming to act out events as realistically as possible. As the narrator describes, the actors visualize movement and action for the audience. In this manner, the narrator is very much like a Greek chorus standing outside the events, but fully describing them.

Props

A traveling bag with *tortillas* in it
A thimble
A brush

A loaf of bread
A second traveling bag

Costumes

See figures 1, 2, 3, 4, and 5 in the introduction to this book.

Cast of Characters

The Narrator

Juanito, *a young man*

The Duende, *a dwarfish, mischievous character who lives in the forest*

Blanca Flor, *a young woman*

Don Ricardo, *an evil man*

Don Ramon, *the father of Juanito*

Doña Arlette, *the mother of Juanito*

Two Doves, *actors in costume*

Scene 1: In the forest.

The Narrator:	*Blanca Flor*, White Flower. There never was a story with such a beautiful name as this story of *Blanca Flor*. At the beginning of our story, a young man named Juanito has left home to seek his fortune in the world. With the blessing of his parents to aid and protect him, he has begun what will be a fantastic adventure. At the beginning of his journey, he wanders into a forest and stops by a stream to rest and eat some of the *tortillas* his mother had packed for his journey.

(Juanito enters and walks around the stage as if looking for a comfortable place to rest. He finally decides upon a spot and sits down. He takes out a tortilla *from his traveling bag and he begins to talk to himself.)*

Juanito:	Whew! I'm hot. This river looks like a good spot to rest for a while. I'm so tired. Maybe this journey wasn't such a good idea. Right now I could be home with *la familia* eating a good supper that *mamacita* cooked for us. But no, I'm out in the world seeking my fortune. So far I haven't found very much, and all I have to show for my efforts are two worn-out feet and a tired body . . . oh, and don't forget (*Holding up a dried* tortilla.) a dried-out *tortilla* . . . (*He quickly looks around as if startled.*) What was that? (*He listens intently and hears a sound again.*) There it is again. I know I heard something . . .

(As Juanito is talking, the Duende enters, sneaking up behind him.)

Juanito:	Must be my imagination. I've been out in the woods too long. You know, if you're alone too long, your mind starts to play tricks on you. Just look at me. I'm talking to my *tortilla* and hearing things . . .
The Duende:	(*In a crackly voice.*) Hello.
Juanito:	Yikes! Who said that! (*He turns around quickly and is startled to see the Duende behind him.*) Who are you?
The Duende:	(*With a mischievous twinkle in his eye.*) Hello.
Juanito:	Hello . . . who, who are you? And where did you come from?

(The Duende grabs the tortilla *out of Juanito's hand and begins to eat it. During the rest of the scene the Duende continues to eat* tortillas.*)*

Juanito:	Hey, that's my *tortilla*.
The Duende:	(*In a playful manner.*) Thank you very much. Thank you very much.
Juanito:	(*To the audience*.) He must be a forest *Duende*. I've heard of them. They're spirits who live in the wood and play tricks on humans. I better go along with him or he might hurt me. (*He offers the Duende another* tortilla. *The*

From ¡*Teatro! Hispanic Plays for Young People.* Copyright © 1996. Teacher Ideas Press. (800) 237-6124.

	Duende takes the tortilla *and begins to eat it, too.*) I hope he's not too hungry. If he eats all my *tortillas*, I won't have any left, and it'll be days before I get food again. I'll have to eat wild berries like an animal. (*He reaches for the* tortilla *and the Duende hits his hand.*) Ouch, that hurt!
The Duende:	Looking for work, eh?
Juanito:	Now I know he's a *Duende*. He can read minds.
The Duende:	No work here. Lost in the forest. No work here.
Juanito:	I know that. We're in the middle of the forest. But I know there'll be work in the next town.
The Duende:	Maybe work right here. Maybe.
Juanito:	Really. Where?

(*The Duende points to a path in the forest. Juan stands up and looks down the path.*)

Juanito:	There's nothing down that path. I've been down that path and there is nothing there.
The Duende:	Look again. Look again. Be careful. Be careful. (*He begins to walk off carrying the bag of* tortillas *with him.*)
Juanito:	Hey, don't leave yet. What type of work? And where? Who do I see? Hey, don't leave yet!
The Duende:	(*The Duende stops and turns.*) Be careful. Danger. Danger. (*He exits.*)
Juanito:	Hey! That's my bag of *tortillas*. Oh this is great. This is really going to sound good when I get back home. My *tortillas*? . . . Oh, they were stolen by a forest *Duende*. Not to worry . . . (*He yells in the direction of the departed Duende.*) And I'm not lost! . . . This is great. Lost and hungry and no work. I guess I'm never going to find my fortune in the world. But what did he mean about work . . . and be careful . . . and danger. I've been down that path and there was nothing there . . . I don't think there was anything there. Oh well, there is only one way to find out. It certainly can't get much worse than things are now, and maybe there is work there.

(*Juanito exits, in the direction of the path the Duende indicated.*)

Scene 2: Farther in the forest.

The Narrator:	In spite of the *Duende*'s warning, Juanito continued on the path of danger. As he came into a clearing, he came to a house and saw a young woman coming out of it.

From *¡Teatro! Hispanic Plays for Young People.* Copyright © 1996. Teacher Ideas Press. (800) 237-6124.

(Juanito enters. Blanca Flor enters from the opposite side of the stage and stops, remaining at the opposite side of the stage.)

Juanito:	Were did this house come from? I was here just yesterday and there was no house here. I must really be lost and turned around. (*He sees the young woman and waves to her.*) Hey! Come here. Over here!

(Blanca Flor runs to Juanito.)

Blanca Flor:	(*With fear in her voice.*) How did you find this place? You must leave right away. The owner of this place is gone, but he will return soon. He leaves to do his work in the world, but he will return unexpectedly. If he finds you here, you'll never be able to leave. You must leave right away.
Juanito:	Why? I haven't done anything.
Blanca Flor:	Please, just leave. And hurry.
Juanito:	Who are you? And why are you here?
Blanca Flor:	I am Blanca Flor. My parents died long ago, and I am kept by this man to pay off their debts to him. I have to work day and night on his farm until I can be free. But he is mean and he has kept prisoner others who have tried to free me. He makes them work until they die from exhaustion.
Juanito:	Who would be so mean?
Blanca Flor:	His name is Don Ricardo.

(Don Ricardo enters, suddenly and with great force.)

Don Ricardo:	(*Addressing Juanito.*) Why are you here! Didn't she tell you to leave!
Blanca Flor:	(*Scared.*) Don't hurt him. He is lost in the forest and got here by mistake. He was just leaving.
Don Ricardo:	Let him answer for himself. Then I will decide what to do with him.
Juanito:	(*Gathering all his courage.*) Yes, she did tell me to leave. But . . . but I am in the world seeking my fortune and I am looking for work. Is there any work for me to do here?
Don Ricardo:	Seeking your fortune! They always say that, don't they, Blanca Flor. Well, I will give you the same chance I have given others. For each of three days, I will give you a job. If in three days you have completed the jobs, then you may leave. If not, then you will work here with me until you are dead. What do you say, fortune-seeker?
Blanca Flor:	(*Pulling Juanito aside.*) Do not say yes. You will never leave here alive. Run and try to escape.
Juanito:	But what about you? You are more trapped than anybody.

From *¡Teatro! Hispanic Plays for Young People.* Copyright © 1996. Teacher Ideas Press. (800) 237-6124.

Blanca Flor:	That is not your worry. Just run and try to escape.
Juanito:	(*Suddenly turning back to Don Ricardo.*) I will do the work you ask.
Don Ricardo:	(*Laughing.*) Blanca Flor, it is always your fault they stay. They all think they will be able to set you free. Well, let's give this one his "fair" chance. (*To Juanito.*) Here is your first job. See that lake over there. Take this thimble (*He gives a thimble to Juanito.*) and use it to carry all the water in the lake to that field over there.
Juanito:	You want me to move a lake with a thimble?!
Don Ricardo:	You wanted work, fortune-seeker. Well, this is your job. Have it finished by morning or your fate will be the same as all the others who tried to save poor Blanca Flor. (*He exits.*)
Juanito:	What type of man is he? I have heard legends of evil men who keep people captive, and in my travels I heard many stories of young men seeking their fortunes who were never seen again, but I always thought they were just stories.
Blanca Flor:	You have had the misfortune to get lost in a terrible part of the forest. Didn't anyone warn you to stay away from here?
Juanito:	Yes . . . one person did. But I thought he was a forest *Duende*, and I didn't really believe him.
Blanca Flor:	It was a forest *Duende*. In this part of the forest there are many creatures with magic. But my keeper, his magic is stronger than any of ours.
Juanito:	Ours? . . . What do you mean ours? Are you part of the magic of this forest?
Blanca Flor:	Do not ask so many questions. The day is passing by, and soon it will be morning.
Juanito:	Morning. I'm supposed to have moved the lake by then. I know this job is impossible, but while God is in his heaven there is a way. I will do this job. And when I am done, I will help you escape from here.

(*Juanito and Blanca Flor exit.*)

Scene 3: The next morning.

(*Juanito and Blanca Flor enter.*)

(*As the narrator speaks, Juanito and Blanca Flor act out the scene as it is described.*)

The Narrator:	Juanito took the thimble and started to carry the water from the lake. He worked as hard as he could, but soon he began to realize that the job really was an impossible one, and he knew he was doomed. He sat down and

From ¡*Teatro! Hispanic Plays for Young People.* Copyright © 1996. Teacher Ideas Press. (800) 237-6124.

began to cry because his luck had abandoned him and because his parent's blessing offered no protection in that evil place. Blanca Flor watched Juanito's valiant effort to move the water. As she watched him crying, her heart was touched and she decided to use her powers to help him. She knew that it was very dangerous to use her powers to help Juanito and to cross Don Ricardo, but she felt it was finally time to end her own torment. As Juanito cried, Blanca Flor took out her brush and began to brush his hair. She cradled Juanito in her arms and her soothing comfort soon put him to sleep . . .

(*As soon as Juanito is asleep, Blanca Flor gently puts his head down and leaves, taking the thimble with her.*)

The Narrator: | When Juanito awoke, he frantically looked for the thimble and, not finding it, ran to the lake. When he reached the lake, he stood at its banks in amazement. All the water was gone. He looked over to the other part of the field, and there stood a lake where before there was nothing. He turned to look for Blanca Flor, but instead there was Don Ricardo.

(*Don Ricardo enters.*)

Don Ricardo: | (*In full force and very angry.*) This must be the work of Blanca Flor, or else you have more power than I thought. I know Blanca Flor is too scared to ever use her powers against me, so as a test of your powers, tomorrow your next job will not be so easy. See that barren ground over on the side of the mountain? You are to clear that ground, plant seeds, grow wheat, harvest it, grind it, cook it, and have bread for me to eat before I return. You still have your life now, but I better have bread tomorrow. (*He exits, with a flourish.*)

(*Juanito exits.*)

Scene 4: The next morning.

(*As the Narrator speaks, Juanito and Blanca Flor enter and act out the scene as it is described.*)

The Narrator: | Immediately upon waking the next morning, Juanito tried to move the rocks in the field, but they were impossible to move because of their great size. Once again, Juanito knew that his efforts were useless. He went over to the new lake and fell down in exhaustion. As he lay in the grass by the lake, Blanca Flor came to him once more and began to brush his hair. Soon, Juanito was asleep.

(*Blanca Flor exits.*)

From *¡Teatro! Hispanic Plays for Young People.* Copyright © 1996. Teacher Ideas Press. (800) 237-6124.

The Narrator:	As before, when he awoke, Juan dashed to the field to make one last attempt to do his work. When he got there, he again stopped in amazement. The field was clear of rocks and the land had been planted and harvested. As he turned around, there stood Blanca Flor.

(Blanca Flor enters.)

Blanca Flor:	(*She hands a loaf of bread to Juanito.*) Give this to Don Ricardo.
Juanito:	How did you do this?

(Don Ricardo enters, quickly.)

Don Ricardo:	What do you have?
Juanito:	(*Shaking with fear.*) Just . . . just this loaf of bread. (*Giving the bread to Don Ricardo.*) Here is the bread you asked for.
Don Ricardo:	(*Very angry.*) This is the work of Blanca Flor. This will not happen again. Tomorrow, your third job will be your final job, and even the powers of Blanca Flor will not help you this time! (*He exits.*)
Blanca Flor:	Believe me, the third job will be impossible to do. It will be too difficult even for my powers. We must run from here if there is to be any chance of escaping his anger. He will kill you because I have helped you. Tonight I will come for you. Be ready to leave quickly as soon as I call for you.

(Juanito and Blanca Flor exit.)

Scene 5: Later that night.

(On one side of the stage, Juanito sits waiting. On the other side, Blanca Flor is in her room grabbing her traveling bag. As she leaves her room, she turns and mimes spitting three times as the narrator describes the action.)

The Narrator:	Late that night, as Juanito waited for her, Blanca Flor packed her belongings into a bag. Before she left the house, she went to the fireplace and spat three times into it.

(Blanca Flor joins Juanito.)

Blanca Flor:	(*Quietly calling.*) Juanito . . . Juanito.
Juanito:	Blanca Flor, is it time?
Blanca Flor:	Yes. We must leave quickly, before he finds out I am gone, or it will be too late.
Juanito:	Won't he know you are gone as soon as he calls for you?

From ¡*Teatro! Hispanic Plays for Young People.* Copyright © 1996. Teacher Ideas Press. (800) 237-6124.

Blanca Flor:	Not right away. I've used my powers to fool him. But it won't last long. Let's go!

(*Juanito and Blanca Flor exit.*)

The Narrator:	When Don Ricardo heard the noise of Juanito and Blanca Flor leaving, he called out . . .
Don Ricardo (*From offstage.*):	Blanca Flor, are you there?
The Narrator:	The spit she had left in the fireplace answered.
Blanca Flor (*From offstage.*):	Yes, I am here.
The Narrator:	Later, Don Ricardo called out again.
Don Ricardo (*From offstage.*):	Blanca Flor, are you there?
The Narrator:	For a second time, the spit she had left in the fireplace answered.
Blanca Flor (*From offstage.*):	Yes, I am here.
The Narrator:	Still later, Don Ricardo called out again, a third time.
Don Ricardo (*From offstage.*):	Blanca Flor, are you there?
The Narrator:	By this time, the fire had evaporated Blanca Flor's spit, and there was no answer. Don Ricardo knew that Blanca Flor was gone, and that she had run away with Juanito. He saddled his horse and galloped up the path to catch them before they escaped from his land.

Scene 6: In the forest.

(*Juanito and Blanca Flor enter, running and out of breath.*)

Juanito:	Blanca Flor, we can rest now. We are free.
Blanca Flor:	No, Juanito, we will not be free until we are beyond the borders of Don Ricardo's land. As long as we are on his land, his powers will work on us.
Juanito:	How much farther?
Blanca Flor:	Remember the river where you met the *Duende*? That river is the border. Across it we are free.
Juanito:	That river is still really far. Let's rest here for a while.
Blanca Flor:	No, he is already after us. We must keep going. I can hear the hooves of his horse.

From ¡*Teatro! Hispanic Plays for Young People.* Copyright © 1996. Teacher Ideas Press. (800) 237-6124.

Juanito:	(*He looks around desperately*.) Where? How can that be?
Blanca Flor:	He is really close. Juanito, come stand by me. Quickly!
Juanito:	(*Still looking around*.) I don't hear anything.
Blanca Flor:	(*Grabbing him and pulling him to her*.) Juanito! Now!

(*As the narrator describes the action, Juanito and Blanca Flor act out the scene. Blanca Flor does not actually throw a brush. She mimes throwing the brush and the action*.)

The Narrator:	Blanca Flor looked behind them and saw that Don Ricardo was getting closer. She reached into her bag, took her brush, and threw it behind her. The brush turned into a church by the side of the road. She then cast a spell on Juanito and turned him into a little old bell ringer. She turned herself into a statue outside the church.

(*Don Ricardo enters, as if riding a horse*.)

Don Ricardo:	(*Addressing the bell ringer [Juanito]*.) Bell ringer, have you seen two young people come this way recently? They would have been in a great hurry and out of breath.
Juanito:	(*In an old man's voice*.) No . . . I don't think so. But maybe last week, two young boys came by. They stopped to pray in the church . . . Or was it two girls. I don't know. I am just an old bell ringer. Not many people actually come by this way at all. You're the first in a long time.
Don Ricardo:	Bell ringer, if you are lying to me you will be sorry. (*He goes over to Blanca Flor [the statue], who is standing very still, as a statue. He examines the statue very closely and then addresses the bell ringer [Juanito]*.) Bell ringer, what saint is this a statue of? The face looks very familiar.
Juanito:	I am an old bell ringer. I don't remember the names of all the saints. But I do know that the statue is very old and has been here a long time. Maybe Saint Theresa or Saint Bernadette.
Don Ricardo:	Bell ringer, if you are lying, I will be back! (*He exits*.)
Juanito:	*Adiós Señor!*

(*Blanca Flor breaks her pose as a statue and goes to Juanito*.)

Blanca Flor:	Juanito, Juanito. The spell is over.
Juanito:	What happened? I did hear the angry hooves of a horse being ridden hard.
Blanca Flor:	We are safe for a while. But he will not give up, and we are not free yet.

(*Juanito and Blanca exit*.)

From *¡Teatro! Hispanic Plays for Young People*. Copyright © 1996. Teacher Ideas Press. (800) 237-6124.

Scene 7: Farther into the forest.

The Narrator:	Blanca Flor and Juanito desperately continued their escape. As they finally stopped for a rest, they had their closest call yet.

(*Blanca Flor and Juanito enter.*)

Juanito:	Blanca Flor, please, let's rest just for a minute.
Blanca Flor:	Okay. We can rest here. I have not heard the hooves of his horse for a while now.
Juanito:	What will he do if he catches us?
Blanca Flor:	He will take us back. I will be watched more closely than ever and you will—
Juanito:	(*Sadly.*) I know. Was there ever a time when you were free? Do you even remember your parents?
Blanca Flor:	Yes. I have the most beautiful memories of my mother, our house, and our animals. Every day, my father would saddle the horses and together we would—
Juanito:	Blanca Flor . . . I hear something.
Blanca Flor:	(*Alarmed.*) He's close. Very close.

(*As the narrator describes the action, Juanito and Blanca Flor act out the scene. Blanca Flor does not actually throw a comb. She mimes throwing the comb and the action.*)

The Narrator:	Blanca Flor quickly opened her bag and threw her comb behind her. Immediately the comb turned into a field of corn. This time she turned Juanito into a scarecrow and she turned herself into a stalk of corn beside him.

(*Don Ricardo enters, as if riding a horse.*)

Don Ricardo:	Where did they go? I still think that the bell ringer knew more than he was saying. They were just here. I could hear their scared little voices. Juanito will pay for this, and Blanca Flor will never have the chance to escape again . . . Now where did they go? Perhaps they are in this field of corn. It is strange to see a stalk of corn grow so close to a scarecrow. But this is a day for strange things. (*He exits.*)
Blanca Flor:	Juanito, it is over again. Let's go. The river is not far. We are almost free.

(*Juanito breaks his pose as a scarecrow and stretches and rubs his legs as Blanca Flor looks around apprehensively.*)

From *¡Teatro! Hispanic Plays for Young People.* Copyright © 1996. Teacher Ideas Press. (800) 237-6124.

| Juanito: | Blanca Flor, that was close. We have to hurry now. The river is just through these trees. We can make it now for sure if we hurry. |
| The Narrator: | But they spoke too soon. Don Ricardo had gotten suspicious about the field of corn and returned to it. When he saw Juanito and Blanca Flor he raced to catch them. |

(*Don Ricardo enters suddenly and sees them.*)

| Don Ricardo: | There you are. I knew something was wrong with that field of corn. Now you are mine. |

(*As the narrator describes the action, Juanito and Blanca Flor act out the scene. Blanca Flor does not actually throw a mirror. She mimes throwing the mirror and the action.*)

| The Narrator: | When Blanca Flor saw Don Ricardo, she reached into her bag and took out a mirror, the final object in the bag. She threw the mirror into the middle of the road. Instantly, the mirror became a large lake, its waters so smooth and still that it looked like a mirror as it reflected the sky and clouds. When Don Ricardo got to the lake, all he saw was two ducks, a male and a female, swimming peacefully in the middle of the lake. Suddenly, the ducks lifted off the lake and flew away. As they flew away, Don Ricardo knew that the ducks were Juanito and Blanca Flor, and that they were beyond his grasp. As they disappeared, he shouted one last curse. |

(*Juanito and Blanca Flor exit.*)

| Don Ricardo: | You may have escaped, Blanca Flor, but you will never have his love. I place a curse on both of you. The first person to embrace him will cause him to forget you forever! (*He exits.*) |

Scene 8: Near Juanito's home.

(*Blanca Flor and Juanito enter.*)

Narrator	Disguised as ducks, Blanca Flor and Juanito flew safely away from that evil land and escaped from Don Ricardo. They finally arrived at Juanito's home, and using Blanca Flor's magical powers, they returned to their human selves.
Juanito:	Blanca Flor, we are close to my home. Soon we will be finally safe forever. I will introduce you to my family and we will begin our new life together . . . Blanca Flor, why do you look so sad? We have escaped the evil Don Ricardo, and soon we will be happy forever.
Blanca Flor:	We have not escaped. His final curse will forever be over us.

From ¡*Teatro! Hispanic Plays for Young People.* Copyright © 1996. Teacher Ideas Press. (800) 237-6124.

Juanito:	Remember, that curse will work only in his own land. You yourself told me that once we were beyond the borders of his land, his powers would have no hold on us.
Blanca Flor:	His powers are very great, Juanito.
Juanito:	Blanca Flor, you have never explained to me the source of your own powers. Are your powers also gone?
Blanca Flor:	The powers have always been in the women of my family. That is why Don Ricardo would not let me leave. He was afraid that I would use my powers against him. I have never been away from that land, so I do not know about my powers in this new land.
Juanito:	You will have no need for your powers here. Soon we will be with my family. Wait outside while I go and tell my family that I have returned from seeking my fortune, safe at last. Then I will tell them that the fortune I found was you.
Blanca Flor:	Juanito, remember the curse.
Juanito:	I am not afraid of any curse. Not with you here with me. All my dreams have come true. Come, let's go meet my family.

(*Juanito and Blanca Flor exit.*)

Scene 9: At Juanito's home.

(*Don Ramon and Doña Arlette are sitting at home passing the time with idle talk.*)

Narrator	Juanito's parents had waited patiently for their son to return from seeking his fortune in the world. They did not know that his return home was only the beginning of another chapter of his great adventure.
Doña Arlette:	Do you ever think we will hear from Juanito? It has been months since he left to seek his fortune in the world?
Don Ramon:	We will hear word soon. I remember when I left home to seek my fortune in the world. Eventually, I found that the best thing to do was return home and make my fortune right here, with my *familia* at my side. Soon he will discover the same thing and you will have your son back.
Doña Arlette:	It is easier for a father to know those things. A mother will never stop worrying about her children.
Don Ramon:	I worry about the children just as much as you do. But there is no stopping children who want to grow up. He has our blessing and permission to go, and that will be what brings him back safe to us. Soon. You just wait.

From *¡Teatro! Hispanic Plays for Young People*. Copyright © 1996. Teacher Ideas Press. (800) 237-6124.

(*Juanito enters. His parents are overjoyed to see him.*)

Juanito:	Mama! Papa! I am home.
Doña Arlette:	¡*Mi jito*!
Don Ramon:	Juanito!

(*Overjoyed with seeing Juanito, his parents rush and embrace him.*)

Doña Arlette:	God has answered my prayers. *Mi jito* has returned home safe.
Don Ramon:	Juanito, come sit close to us and tell us all about your adventures in the world. What great adventures did you have?
Juanito:	I had the greatest adventures. For the longest time I was unlucky and unable to find work but finally I . . . I . . .
Doña Arlette:	What is it? Are you okay? Do you need some food?
Juanito:	No, I'm okay. It's just that I was going to say something and I forgot what I was going to say.
Don Ramon:	Don't worry. If it is truly important, it'll come back.
Juanito:	No, I've definitely forgotten what I was going to say. Oh well, it probably wasn't important anyway.
Doña Arlette:	Did you meet someone special? Did you bring a young woman back for us to meet?
Juanito:	No, I didn't have those kind of adventures. Pretty much nothing happened and then I finally decided that it was just best to come home.
Don Ramon:	(*To Doña Arlette.*) See what I told you? That is exactly what I said would happen.
Doña Arlette:	Now that you are home, it is time to settle down and start your own family. You know our neighbor Don Emilio has a young daughter who would make a very good wife. Perhaps we should go visit her family this Sunday.
Juanito:	You know, that would probably be a good idea. I must admit that I was hoping I would find love on my adventures, but I have come home with no memories of love at all. Perhaps it is best to make my fortune right here, close to home.
Don Ramon:	(*To Doña Arlette.*) See? That is exactly what I said would happen.

(*All exit.*)

From ¡*Teatro! Hispanic Plays for Young People.* Copyright © 1996. Teacher Ideas Press. (800) 237-6124.

Scene 10: Months later at Juanito's home.

The Narrator: Blanca Flor had seen the embrace and knew that the evil curse had been fulfilled. Brokenhearted, she traveled to a nearby village and lived there in hopes that one day the curse could be broken. The people of the village soon got to know Blanca Flor and came to respect her for the good person she was. One day, Blanca Flor heard news that a celebration was being held in honor of Juanito's return home. She immediately knew that this might be her one chance to break the curse. From the times when she had brushed Juanito's hair, she had kept a lock of his hair. She took one strand of his hair and made it into a dove. She then took one stand of her own hair and turned it into another dove. She took these two doves to Juanito's celebration as a present.

(*Juanito and Don Ramon are sitting talking.*)

Don Ramon: Juanito, what was the most fantastic thing that happened on your adventures?

Juanito: Really father, nothing much at all happened. Sometimes I begin to have a memory of something, but it never becomes really clear. At night I have these dreams, but when I awake in the morning I cannot remember them. It must be some dream I keep trying to remember . . . or forget.

Don Ramon: I remember when I went into the world to seek my fortune. I was a young man like you . . .

(*Doña Arlette enters.*)

Doña Arlette: Juanito, there's a young woman here with a present for you.

Juanito: Who is it?

Doña Arlette: I don't really know her. She is the new young woman who just recently came to the village. The women of the church say she is constantly doing good works for the church and that she is a very good person. She has brought you a present to help celebrate your coming home safe.

Juanito: Sure. Let her come in.

(*Blanca Flor enters with the two Doves. The Doves are actors in costume, see figure 6 in introduction.*)

Blanca Flor: (*Speaking to Juanito.*) Thank you for giving me the honor of presenting these doves as gifts to you.

Juanito: No. No. The honor is mine. Thank you. They are very beautiful.

Blanca Flor: They are special doves. They are singing doves.

Doña Arlette: I have never heard of singing doves before. Where did you get them?

From *¡Teatro! Hispanic Plays for Young People.* Copyright © 1996. Teacher Ideas Press. (800) 237-6124.

Blanca Flor:	They come from a special place. A place where all things have a magic power. There are no other doves like these in the world.
Don Ramon:	Juanito, what a gift! Let's hear them sing!
Doña Arlette:	Yes, let's hear them sing.
Blanca Flor:	(*To Juanito.*) May they sing to you?
Juanito:	Yes, of course. Let's hear their song.

(*Everyone sits to listen to the Doves' song. As the Doves begin to chant, their words begin to have a powerful effect on Juanito. His memory of Blanca Flor returns to him.*)

Doves:	Once there was a faraway land A land of both good and evil powers. A river flowed at the edge like a steady hand And it was guarded by a *Duende* for all the hours. Of all the beautiful things the land did hold The most beautiful with the purest power Was a young maiden, true and bold Named Blanca Flor, the White Flower.
Juanito:	I remember! The doves' song has made me remember. (*Going to Blanca Flor.*) Blanca Flor, your love has broken the curse. Now I remember all that was struggling to come out. Mama, Papa, here is Blanca Flor, the love I found when I was seeking my fortune.

(*Juanito and Blanca Flor embrace.*)

Don Ramon:	This is going to be a really good story!

(*All exit with Juanito stopping to give Blanca Flor a big hug.*)

From *¡Teatro! Hispanic Plays for Young People.* Copyright © 1996. Teacher Ideas Press. (800) 237-6124.

El Muchacho que Mato al Gigante
The Boy Who Killed the Giant

Introduction

The Boy Who Killed the Giant is a wonderful adventure story with many characteristics of what is known in folklore terms as an "ordinary" story. Of course the story in itself is not "ordinary." Folklorists have identified this category in this manner because there are so many stories with these characteristics that the stories, as a group, become "ordinary."

The characteristics of these stories are far from "ordinary," however. The central event is the common deed of rescuing a princess from a giant. The rescuer, usually a young boy seeking adventure, receives help from unexpected sources. In this version of the story, the help comes from the animal kingdom. The magical statements of the animals are one of the elements giving this story its Hispanic identification.

Staging

The most challenging aspect of staging this story is the task of creating animal characters. It is not necessary to strive for realism when creating animals portrayed by actors. Most important is that the actor create one identifying stance, movement, or posture that is clearly identifying of the animal. Improvisational movement games will help actors discover movements that will create the animal for the audience. At the beginning of the play Diego must visibly grow older three times. The actor playing Diego can indicate this aging with a change of hats or T-shirts appropriate to each age level.

The thunder and lightning at the end of the play can be realized with special effects tapes or by the traditional theatrical effect of shaking a large piece of sheet metal off-stage.

Props

A magic pouch	An eagle feather	A golden egg
A traveling bag	A greyhound hair	Bags of gold
A bear claw	A lion hair	

Costumes

See figures 1, 2, 4, 5, and 6 in the introduction to this book.

Cast of Characters

The Narrator	The Old Woman
Diego, *a young boy*	The Princess
Papa, *the father of Diego*	The Giant
Mama, *the mother of Diego*	The Beast in the Lake
The Bear	The Rabbit in the Beast
The Eagle	The Bird in the Rabbit
The Dog, *a greyhound*	The King
The Lion	The King's servants

Scene 1: At the farm of a young boy, Diego.

The Narrator: | Many years ago, in a distant land, there lived a boy who thought he was old enough to leave home and seek his fortune in the world. He gathered up his belongings and went to his parents to ask for their blessing for his journey.

(*Diego, Papa, and Mama enter.*)

Diego: | Mama, Papa, may I have your blessing to go into the world and seek my fortune?

Mama: | Oh no, Diego. You are much too young to leave home. Go outside and play with your toys.

(*Diego exits, sulking. His parents remain on stage.*)

The Narrator: | A full year passes, and the little boy really felt he was old enough to leave home. He approached his parents again and asked for their blessing.

(*Diego enters.*)

Diego: | Mama, Papa, I am a year older now. All the other boys have left home to seek their fortune in the world. Please, may I have your blessing for my journey?

Papa: | Diego, I know your friends are leaving, but it is not time for you to go yet. You are still a child. Now go and play with your toys. Maybe later, when you are older.

(*Diego exits, sulking. His parents remain on stage.*)

The Narrator: | Another year passed and the boy was finally turning into a young man. This time, even his parents knew that it was time for him to leave home and seek his fortune in the world.

(*Diego enters.*)

Diego: | Mama, Papa. I am leaving home. May I have your blessing?

Mama: | You have our blessing. Remember that if you are ever in trouble, call on the blessing we give you today and you will be safe.

Papa: | And if you do find your fortune, come back and tell us about your great adventures.

(*All exit.*)

From *¡Teatro! Hispanic Plays for Young People.* Copyright © 1996. Teacher Ideas Press. (800) 237-6124.

Scene 2: In a field.

(*Diego enters.*)

(*As the narrator speaks, Diego carefully attaches his magic pouch to his belt.*)

The Narrator:	Overjoyed with the prospect of finally beginning his adventures, Diego packed his belongings in his traveling bag. He was especially careful to include his magic pouch. All his childhood he had kept his magic pouch on his belt and whenever he found something magic, he would put it into his belt for safekeeping. He finally waved good-bye to his parents and began his journey. He had only been gone a few hours when he came over a hill and saw a most amazing sight.
Diego:	I wonder what this day holds for me. I hope I am lucky and find my fortune really soon. As soon as I have made my fortune in the world, I am going to return home and give my parents the life they deserve. Their whole life has been one of sacrifice for *la familia*. One day I will be the provider for the family. Then they will get the rest they deserve.

(*As Diego finishes speaking, the Bear, the Eagle, the Dog, and the Lion enter. The animals are engaged in a fierce battle.*)

The Bear:	The animal is mine!
The Lion:	Mine!
The Dog:	This animal is mine, no matter what you all say!
The Eagle:	The animal is mine!

(*Diego rushes into the midst of the animals and tries to stop the argument.*)

Diego:	Wait! Stop! What are you fighting about? Someone is going to get hurt.
The Bear:	I am the strongest of all the animals. The dead animal we have found is mine to eat.
The Lion:	I am king of the beasts. I deserve to eat this animal.
The Dog:	Because of my great speed, I was the first one to get to the animal. I was already eating it when all of you showed up. The animal is mine.
The Eagle:	I am the fiercest hunter of the skies. I saw the animal first. The animal is mine!

(*The animals renew their fighting, each protesting why it deserves the animal.*)

From *¡Teatro! Hispanic Plays for Young People.* Copyright © 1996. Teacher Ideas Press. (800) 237-6124.

Diego:	Stop! This is no way to settle an argument. In my world, the human world, we use cooperation to solve fights. Just listen to my plan and all of you will end up happy instead of angry. Listen, this is what you should do. Divide the animal into four pieces. Then each of you will get a share of the meat. This is the only way to solve this argument.
The Narrator:	The animals did as Diego had advised them. When they were finished eating, they spoke to Diego.
The Lion:	We have never seen a boy so brave as to step into the middle of four angry animals fighting.
The Bear:	Or so wise as to come up with such a simple but perfect solution to an argument.
The Eagle:	We have talked among ourselves and we have decided that because you have been so brave and wise—
The Dog:	We will each give you a reward.
The Lion:	(*Pulling a golden strand of hair from his mane.*) Here is a strand of golden hair from my mane. If you ever need my help, cry out "*A Dios y León*" to God and the Lion, and I will be your fiercest fighter.
The Bear:	(*Pulling a claw off his hand.*) Here is a claw from my hand. If you ever need my help, cry out "*A Dios y Oso*" to God and the Bear, and I will be your mightiest defender.
The Dog:	(*Pulling a long grey hair from his tail.*) Here is a grey hair from my tail. If you ever need my help, cry out "*A Dios y Perro*" to God and the Dog, and I will be your swiftest helper.
The Eagle:	(*Pulling a feather from his tail.*) Here is the most precious object I can give you. Here is the sacred eagle feather. If you ever need my help, cry out "*A Dios y Águila*" to God and the Eagle, and I will be at your side.

(*Diego takes the gifts and carefully places each in his magic pouch on his belt. The animals all exit with a flourish.*)

Diego:	I can't believe my good fortune. I've only been gone from home for a few hours and already I am beginning to collect my fortune. If only my parents could see me now. Four magic things already! (*He exits.*)

Scene 3: The King's castle.

The Narrator:	After carefully putting away his treasures in his magic pouch, Diego bid the animals farewell, never expecting to see them again, and he continued on his journey. Soon he came upon the castle of the King. He had never been away from home, and he was very surprised to find the King's castle so close to home.

From *¡Teatro! Hispanic Plays for Young People.* Copyright © 1996. Teacher Ideas Press. (800) 237-6124.

(*Diego enters, looking about as if he is seeing something immense.*)

Diego:	Wow. The King's castle. And so close to home. I wonder why my parents never told me about this. I can't wait to get home and tell everyone how big it is. Look at these doors. They . . . (*Pushing against the doors.*) They're not locked. They just came right open. (*Looking around.*) And where are the guards? Where is everybody? (*Yelling out.*) Hello . . . Hello!

(*The Old Woman enters, shuffling and crying. Diego see the woman and addresses her.*)

Diego:	Excuse me, *Señora*. Why are you crying? And where is everybody?
The Old Woman:	Haven't you heard? The Giant has stolen the Princess. The King has sent all of his bravest and strongest soldiers to save the Princess, but the Giant has killed all of them.
Diego:	All of them? And where did he take the Princess?
The Old Woman:	There is no one left to save the Princess. She is prisoner of the Giant in his castle far away from here. On top of a barren and treacherous mountain, where no man can save her. Now we know that we will never see her again. That is why all the people of the castle spend all their days crying.
Diego:	I am in the world seeking my fortune, and I just received four magic treasures from the animals. I know I can save the Princess.
The Old Woman:	Oh little boy, the Giant has already killed all the King's men. You are too young and small to be of any help. Go play with your little magic toys.
Diego:	No really, my friends will come and help. We can save the Princess.
The Old Woman:	I wish you could. The Princess was all that was bright and good about the castle. Now that she is gone a sadness is in the King's heart that will never be lifted. I wish I weren't so old, that I could still believe in the help of magic friends.
Diego:	My friends are regular animals. They said that all I had to do was call them and—
The Old Woman:	The dreams of childhood. The Princess used to play the same imaginary games. Go, little boy. Play your games. It's the only happiness we will ever know now. (*She exits.*)
Diego:	(*Sadly.*) I wish I could help the Princess. She's probably right. Now I'll never find my fortune, and the Princess will never be rescued. Oh now I wish I'd never left home. (*He exits.*)

From ¡*Teatro! Hispanic Plays for Young People*. Copyright © 1996. Teacher Ideas Press. (800) 237-6124.

Scene 4: At the Giant's castle.

(*Diego enters.*)

The Narrator: | Late that night, Diego was trying to fall asleep underneath a tree in a field outside the castle when he heard the saddest song. Far off in the distance, he could see the Giant's castle on top of a scary mountain. The singing voice was the Princess, carried by the gentle night breeze all the way to Diego's ears. The song was so sad that the little boy knew that he just had to do something, no matter what the old woman had said.

Diego: | (*He reaches into his magic pouch and pulls out the eagle feather. Holding it up, he cries out.*) A Dios y Águila, to God and the Eagle!

(*As the narrator describes the action, the Eagle swoops in and carries off Diego.*)

The Narrator: | As soon as he had cried out, the eagle swooped down and carried off Diego. The eagle knew just what Diego wanted. It flew the little boy to the Giant's castle, right into the room where the Princess was being held prisoner in a room in the Giant's castle.

(*Diego and the Eagle exit. The Princess enters stage center and mimes holding onto bars as if she is jailed inside a cage. When she is in position, Diego and the Eagle enter flying around the Princess. The Eagle deposits Diego by the Princess and exits.*)

The Princess: | Whoever you are, and however you got here, run away! If the Giant sees you, he will kill you! And by the way, how did you get here?

Diego: | My friend the eagle brought me here. The old woman told me what happened and I know I can help you.

The Princess: | No one can help me. The Giant is the most powerful creature on earth.

(*Suddenly, a series of very loud booms are heard off-stage as the Giant approaches. The Giant enters. As he enters, the Princess shrinks in fear and Diego scurries and hides at the edge of the stage.*)

The Giant: | (*In a booming voice.*) Who has been here?!

The Princess: | No one, Giant. No one.

The Giant: | Good! Because if someone was here, I would have to kill him!

The Princess: | No one is here, Giant. You've already killed all my father's soldiers. No one is left who could save me.

(*The Giant exits, with an evil laugh echoing as he leaves.*)

From *¡Teatro! Hispanic Plays for Young People.* Copyright © 1996. Teacher Ideas Press. (800) 237-6124.

Diego:	(*Coming out of hiding*.) Boy is he big. And mean. And stinky!
The Princess:	Oh I wish you could save me. But you had better run as fast as you can before the Giant finds you. Please go and save yourself.
Diego:	No, I can help you. I really can.
The Princess:	How can you save me? You are just a little boy.
Diego:	But I have friends. Powerful and magical friends.
The Princess:	Where are they?
Diego:	They only come if I call them. They gave me magic treasures. But first we must find out where the Giant keeps his powers. Trick him into telling you where he keeps his powers. Then I will be able to destroy his powers.
The Princess:	Oh you will never kill the Giant. I have seen how powerful he is. You will . . . Oh here he comes again. Run and hide quickly before he gets you!

(*Again a loud booming is heard off-stage as the Giant approaches. The Giant enters and again Diego hides at the edge of the stage.*)

The Giant:	(*In his booming, gruff voice*.) Who were you talking to?!
The Princess:	No one, Giant. I get so lonely here by myself. I just talk to the birds that fly by the window.
The Giant:	Good. You might as well get used to things here, because it will never change.
The Princess:	That's not true. One day someone will come and save me.
The Giant:	No one will ever save you! They have already tried and tried, and you know what happened to them all.
The Princess:	One day someone is going to come and find your powers and destroy them!
The Giant:	That will never happen! And you know why. On a mountain far away from here, too far for any person to get to, there is a lake on fire. And if you could get to that lake, which you can't, in that lake is a beast. A giant, powerful, ferocious beast. And if you could kill that beast, which you can't, you would have to cut through seven layers of hide. And if you could cut through those seven layers of hide, which you can't, inside that beast is a rabbit. And if you could catch that rabbit, which you can't, inside that rabbit is a bird. And if you could catch that bird, which you can't, inside that bird is an egg. And if you could get that egg, which you can't, inside that egg are my powers! And that is why no one will ever get to my powers! They are safe forever! (*He laughs his crazy, evil laugh.*)
The Princess:	I will never give up hope! One day I will be free!

From ¡*Teatro! Hispanic Plays for Young People*. Copyright © 1996. Teacher Ideas Press. (800) 237-6124.

The Giant:	Dream on, Princess. But don't even begin to believe you will ever leave this castle, because you won't! (*He exits.*)
The Princess:	
Diego:	(*Coming out from hiding.*) You were really brave. I was scared to death he would find out about your trick.
The Princess:	He really believes no one will ever get his powers.
Diego:	Remember, I am not alone. I have my friends. Wish me luck! (*He reaches into his magic pouch and pulls out the eagle feather. Holding it up, he cries out.*) A Dios y Águila, to God and the Eagle!

(*The Eagle comes and flies away with Diego. The Princess exits.*)

Scene 5: At the lake.

(*Diego enters.*)

| The Narrator: | When the eagle had flown Diego to the lake, he saw why the Giant was so sure no one would ever get to the beast in the lake. The lake was in the middle of a volcano, which was about to erupt. The lake was on fire with molten lava spewing out of the earth. As he approached the lake, the ground started trembling as if an earthquake were coming. Suddenly, the beast rose out of the middle of the lake. |
| Diego: | The lake is on fire! And why is the ground shaking so much? |

(*The Beast in the Lake enters.*)

| Diego: | Help! (*Diego reaches into his magic pouch and pulls out the lion hair. Holding it up, he cries out.*) A Dios y León, to God and the Lion! |

(*The Lion enters.*)

(*As the narrator speaks, the actors mime the action.*)

| The Narrator: | As if out of nowhere, the lion appeared and began to fight with the beast. They fought a fierce life and death struggle. Finally, the beast picked up the lion and started to crush it to death. |
| Diego: | Oh no! The beast is too strong for the lion. I can't let my friend the lion be killed. (*He reaches into his magic pouch and pulls out the bear claw. Holding it up, he cries out.*) A Dios y Oso, to God and the Bear! |

(*The Bear enters.*)

| The Narrator: | As if by magic, the bear appeared and began to fight with the beast. The fight was desperate and ferocious. Finally, the bear lifted the beast and crushed it dead. The lion and the bear collapsed in exhaustion by the beast. Following the Giant's instructions, Diego took out his knife and began to cut through the seven layers of hide on the beast. |

From ¡Teatro! Hispanic Plays for Young People. Copyright © 1996. Teacher Ideas Press. (800) 237-6124.

Diego:	One, two, three, four, five, six, seven!
The Narrator:	As Diego cut through the seventh layer of hide, a rabbit bolted out and began to run away. Diego tried as hard as he could to catch the rabbit, but the rabbit was too fast.
Diego:	I'll never catch the rabbit. It's too fast . . . the dog! Why didn't I think of it sooner. (*He reaches into his magic pouch and pulls out the dog hair. Holding it up, he cries out.*) A Dios y Perro, to God and the Dog!

(*The Dog enters.*)

The Narrator:	Immediately, the dog appeared and caught the rabbit. As the dog caught the rabbit, a bird flew out of the rabbit and flew away.
Diego:	This is the easiest one yet! (*He reaches into his magic pouch and pulls out the eagle feather. Holding it up, he cries out.*) A Dios y Águila, to God and the Eagle!

(*The Eagle enters.*)

The Narrator:	Immediately, the eagle appeared and caught the bird. As the eagle caught the bird, it dropped a golden egg. Diego caught the egg and held it up for all to see.
Diego:	My friends, in this egg are the powers of the Giant!

(*All exit.*)

Scene 6: At the Giant's castle.

(*The Princess enters. She sits in her room.*)

The Narrator:	Diego had been gone so long that the Princess had begun to give up hope of ever being saved. Each passing day was marked with the frightening visits from the Giant.

(*Loud booming is heard off-stage as the Giant approaches. The Giant enters.*)

The Giant:	So Princess, no one came to save you today! (*He laughs his cruel and evil laugh.*) Too bad. Maybe tomorrow.
The Princess:	Yes, maybe tomorrow. Or the day after that. Or after that!
The Giant:	I hope someone comes soon. I'm getting bored with nothing to do. It was much more fun when your father was sending men to save you all the time. I shouldn't have killed them all so fast. Or I should have thrown a few in my dungeons so I could take them out now to have something to do.

From ¡*Teatro! Hispanic Plays for Young People*. Copyright © 1996. Teacher Ideas Press. (800) 237-6124.

The Princess:	All over the kingdom, my father is gathering a new army to attack your castle.
The Giant:	Really! That's the best news I've heard yet. This time I will throw a few in the dungeons.
The Princess:	This army will destroy your castle!
The Giant:	If they don't come soon, I'm going to have to steal another princess just to have something to do. Then you'll have a little playmate so you won't be so lonely. Two princesses. Two armies trying to save them. The dungeons full. You've given me a good idea, Princess. I was beginning to think you were not worth the trouble. Your father had so few men that the fighting was over too fast. Next time, I'm stealing only princesses whose fathers have large armies. (*He exits, laughing.*)
The Princess:	I am doomed. And now another princess will be stolen and the Giant will kill even more men. By now the beast in the lake has killed that poor little boy.

(*As the Princess speaks, the Eagle and Diego enter, flying in, returning from the lake.*)

The Princess:	You're back! I'd given up all hope.
Diego:	Look what I have. (*He shows her the golden egg.*)
The Princess:	The egg! How did you get it!
Diego:	I didn't. My friends got it for me.
The Princess:	But the beast.
Diego:	My friends killed it. The lion and the bear fought with it, and the bear killed it. It was just like the Giant said it would be. (*He mimes cutting through the seven layers of hide.*) One, two, three, four, five, six, seven! And then the rabbit came out, and then the bird. And here is the egg. Inside it are the Giant's powers.

(*As Diego mentions the egg, a loud booming is heard off-stage as the Giant approaches. Diego takes the egg and hides at the edge of the stage as the Giant enters.*)

The Giant:	Princess, I'm off to steal me another princess. Soon the good old days will be back again. Men storming the castle. Me killing them. I can't wait. Now don't you go anywhere while I'm gone . . . Who's been here?
The Princess:	(*Very nervous.*) No one. No one at all.
The Giant:	Someone has been here! I can smell him. (*He begins to search the stage.*)
The Princess:	Little boy run! The Giant knows you're here!

From *¡Teatro! Hispanic Plays for Young People.* Copyright © 1996. Teacher Ideas Press. (800) 237-6124.

(*The Giant discovers Diego hiding.*)

The Giant: | Now you will die like all the rest!

(*As the Giant reaches for Diego, Diego holds out the egg.*)

The Giant: | Where did you get that egg! That's not the egg with my powers in it, so you might as well just give it to me.

Diego: | The beast is dead.

The Giant: | My beast is dead!

The Princess: | And soon you'll be dead, Giant!

The Giant: | Give me that egg!

(*The Giant and Diego slowly circle each other. Diego holds on tightly to the egg.*)

The Giant: | Give me that egg! I said give me that egg!

(*In a desperate move, Diego hurls the egg at the Giant. As the egg hits the Giant in the head, the room fills with thunder and lightning. When all the thunder has stopped, the Giant falls to the ground, dead.*)

The Princess: | Is he dead?

(*Diego carefully examines the fallen Giant.*)

Diego: | Yes. He's dead.

(*All exit.*)

Scene 7: At the King's castle.

The Narrator: | At the King's castle, life had continued in its sad way. The King was desperately trying to gather a new army, but the men were afraid to join it because they heard what had happened to the first army. One day the old woman was walking in the courtyard when she looked up and she saw an amazing sight. The eagle was flying into the castle, and on its back were Diego and the Princess. The old woman ran and told the King that the Princess had been saved.

(*Diego, the Princess, the Old Woman, and the King enter.*)

The Old Woman: | (*To the King.*) It's the little boy I told you about. He saved the Princess.

Diego: | I told you I could save the Princess. My friends helped me just like I said they would.

From *¡Teatro! Hispanic Plays for Young People*. Copyright © 1996. Teacher Ideas Press. (800) 237-6124.

The Old Woman:	From now on, I will always believe in the power of magical friends.
The King:	(*To Diego*.) You have brought sunshine and joy back to my kingdom. You have done what all my men could not do. Because of your bravery, I will give you a great reward. I will give you gold beyond your imagination.

(*The King gestures and his servants enter, bringing bags filled with gold.*)

The King:	Take these. There is no reward I can give you as precious as the life of my daughter. But take this gold to make your life and your family's life better. And know that I am forever grateful to you, and that you, your family, and your descendants will always be welcome to feast at my table. Go now, and know that the gates of my castle will always open for you.
Diego:	(*To the Princess*.) I'm glad I was able to help you.
The Princess:	(*She kisses Diego*.) Thank you with all my heart.

(*All exit.*)

Scene 8: At Diego's home.

(*Mama and Papa enter.*)

The Narrator:	While he had been away, Diego's parents had worried and wondered about Diego and his travels. They prayed for the day when Diego would return home. One day, as they were working in the field, they looked up and saw Diego walking down the path to their farm, carrying the bags of gold.

(*Diego enters.*)

Mama:	Diego!
Papa:	Diego!
Diego:	Mama! Papa!

(*All embrace.*)

Mama:	My prayers are answered. You have returned home safe.
Papa:	And what is in these bags?
Diego:	Open them and look.

(*Diego's parents open the bags and look in. They run their hands through the gold.*)

Mama:	How did you get all this gold?

(*Diego mimes talking to his parents, as his parents listen.*)

From ¡Teatro! Hispanic Plays for Young People. Copyright © 1996. Teacher Ideas Press. (800) 237-6124.

The Narrator:	And so Diego told his parents of his adventures since he had left home. He told them about the four fighting animals. He told them about the four magic gifts. He told them about the King's castle. But most of all, he told them about the Princess. And the Giant. And the egg. His parents were amazed by the story of his adventures. After they heard the stories, they told Diego . . .
Mama:	We are so glad you came home safe after your great adventures.
Papa:	And if you ever want to go into the world again to seek your fortune . . . go right ahead!

From *¡Teatro! Hispanic Plays for Young People*. Copyright © 1996. Teacher Ideas Press. (800) 237-6124.

Juan Oso
John the Bear

Introduction

Juan Oso, John the Bear, is a story about a fabled youth with the strength of a bear. The traditional versions of this story all have John having a bear as his father. These versions also contain the defining story elements of the rescue of princesses, the traditional marriage to a princess, and the happily-ever-after ending. A unique element of this story is the betrayal by trusted companions. The names of the companions vary from version to version, but they all are names referring to some type of mastery of natural forces.

Staging

The staging of this story is fairly straightforward when compared to stories with more elements of magic and transformation. All the characters in the story are recognizable humans with no special powers. Even the two strong companions do not actually perform magical feats in the story. Their accomplishments are the product of their great strength.

Props

Camp cooking pan

Two gems

Princess crowns

Costumes

See figures 1, 2, 4, and 5 in the introduction to this book.

Cast of Characters

The Narrator

Juan Oso, *a young man with the strength of a bear*

Patricia, *the mother of Juan Oso*

Mudarríos, *River Mover*

Mudacerros, *Mountain Mover*

The Duende, *a dwarfish, mischievous character who lives in the forest*

Princess #1

Princess #2

Princess #3

The King

The Queen

The King's Guards

Scene 1: At the house of Juan Oso.

The Narrator: At the beginning of this story we meet Juan Oso, John the Bear. He is called John the Bear because of his great strength. In his childhood, people recognized that his strength was greater than any other child. As he grew, his strength was more than any man's. In time, he gained the reputation for having the strength of a bear, and soon gained the name of Juan Oso, John the Bear.

(*Patricia enters.*)

Patricia: (*Calling out.*) Juan. Juan Oso. You come here this minute!

(*Juan enters.*)

Juan: I'm right over here. What's wrong?

Patricia: What's wrong? Everything is wrong. I just got back from the church and the *padre* had a little talk with me.

Juan: What about?

Patricia: What else? You.

Juan: Mama, you know not to believe everything the *padre* says. Especially about me.

Patricia: Juan, this is the third time he has had this talk with me, and this is the third time we have had to have this talk. And you know what it is about.

Juan: What?

Patricia: You know what. The same thing it has been the last two times. Your strength.

Juan: Mama, I'm not to blame for my strength. I was born this way. The other kids even joke that my father was a bear, and that this is why I have my strength.

Patricia: Juan, you have to stop using your strength to show off. You're starting to hurt other kids, and their parents are complaining.

Juan: We're just playing. And the other kids are always asking me to use my strength. They like to see it.

Patricia: From the time you were born, we all could see your great strength. When you were young, it was cute. But now that you are almost a man, people are afraid of your strength.

Juan: My strength is the best thing I could have for the work on the farm. You yourself have told me that many times.

From ¡*Teatro! Hispanic Plays for Young People*. Copyright © 1996. Teacher Ideas Press. (800) 237-6124.

Patricia:	Juan, something has to be done. One day, you really are going to hurt someone and, play or not, you will be in a lot of trouble.
Juan:	What am I supposed to do, Mama? I just play, and my strength is so great that something always happens.
Patricia:	Juan, I never thought I would be the one to say this. Usually, it is the child who brings it up first. But now you are almost grown, and I think it is time you go into the world to find adventure and to seek your fortune.
Juan:	I don't want to go into the world. Please don't send me away.
Patricia:	I'm not sending you away. Even if you had never had your strength, this time would have come. Sooner or later, every child must go into the world to seek his fortune. Now it is your turn.
Juan:	Perhaps it is for the best. My strength has made me different all my life. Perhaps in my adventures my strength will be something to bring me good fortune.
Patricia:	Juan, you have my blessing on your journeys, and I know that, in the world, your great strength will protect you and bring you good fortune.

(*They embrace and exit.*)

Scene 2: In the forest.

| The Narrator: | And so began the great adventures of Juan Oso, John the Bear. As expected, wherever he went, Juan was able to find work. His great strength made him the most respected of all the workers in the land. In his travels, however, he soon began to hear the legends of two men whose strength was as great as his. He had never imagined that there could be someone as strong as he was. But soon he was to find out that his was not the only great strength in the world. |

(*Mudarríos enters. He busies himself digging a giant hole in the ground. All action is mimed.*)

| Mudarríos: | (*Singing to himself.*) From early in the morn Since the very day I was born Till the end of night I have had to work with all my might. There has never been a man as mighty as me I have searched the earth from sea to sea And everywhere I look still I have not found A man such as me who could move a river from its ground. |

From *¡Teatro! Hispanic Plays for Young People.* Copyright © 1996. Teacher Ideas Press. (800) 237-6124.

(As Mudarríos is singing Juan enters and listens to his song.)

Juan:	*(Answering in song.)* Your boasts are like water filled with sand Shallow and easily disturbed by another hand Until now you say you have always ruled the day But before my strength you should move and clear the way.

(Mudarríos turns and approaches Juan. As they speak, Juan and Mudarríos circle each other like two wary animals.)

Mudarríos:	Who are you to challenge me in this way?
Juan:	Juan Oso, John the Bear.
Mudarríos:	I am Mudarríos, River Mover.
Juan:	My strength is as great as the bear.
Mudarríos:	My strength allows me to move rivers from where they run.
Juan:	Then we shall see who is to be called the strongest of men at the end of this day.
Mudarríos:	We shall see.

(Juan and Mudarríos lock arms in a wrestling grip. They grapple in a fight similar to arm wrestling, but standing up. They are evenly matched, and the tide of the fight switches back and forth between them. First it seems as if Juan might win. Then it seems as if Mudarríos might win. Finally, both give up because the struggle is so evenly matched.)

Juan:	An even match!
Mudarríos:	Even and well fought!
Juan:	I am on my journeys in the world seeking adventure and my fortune.
Mudarríos:	I am wandering the earth finding what work I can. I am called Mudarríos, River Mover, because that is the work I do best. Almost all the rivers of the earth have been moved by me. I always find the best path for the river as it seeks its way back home to the great ocean.
Juan:	My work has been very much the same. I have cleared forests in one day. I have moved houses to the top of the mountain. I have carried horses across raging rivers to safety.
Mudarríos:	River Mover and John the Bear. Finally I have found a *compadre* to share my work.
Juan:	And I have found a friend whose strength is as great as mine.

From *¡Teatro! Hispanic Plays for Young People.* Copyright © 1996. Teacher Ideas Press. (800) 237-6124.

Mudarríos:	I must tell you, there is one other whose strength is equal to ours. His name is Mudacerros, Mountain Mover. Often, when I am doing the job of moving the river, I have seen Mudacerros across the valley doing his work of moving the mountain.
Juan:	How could one man's strength be so great that it moves mountains?
Mudarríos:	If you listen, you will hear the footsteps of Mudacerros. He was working close to me this morning, and the shaking of the ground tells me that he will soon be here.

(The approaching footsteps of Mudacerros are heard off-stage. They have the loud booming of a giant approaching. Mudacerros enters. He goes over to Mudarríos and gives him a hearty slap on the back.)

Mudacerros:	Mudarríos! My old friend. I saw you working in the other valley this morning. How many rivers have you moved today?
Mudarríos:	Too many. One I put right on top of the land where you had just moved a mountain.
Mudacerros:	And who is our good friend here?
Juan:	I am Juan Oso, John the Bear.
Mudarríos:	His strength is as great as ours. He matched me pull-for-pull in an arm fight. And I must admit, he almost beat me.
Mudacerros:	*(He gives Juan a hearty slap on the back.)* Juan Oso, join us in our work. No man will be able to match the work we three will be able to do. River Mover. Mountain Mover. And John the Bear!
Mudarríos:	With you working beside us, all the work of the world will be ours.
Juan:	Then I truly have found my fortune. When I left home, I knew that my strength would help me find my good fortune, and it has.
Mudarríos:	*Compadres*, let's begin our journeys. The work of the world waits for us.

(All exit.)

Scene 3: At a camp in the forest.

The Narrator:	Juan had found his good fortune. He was never without work, and he enjoyed the company of his two friends Mudarríos and Mudacerros. One night, as they were camping, they had a strange visitor, a *Duende*, a forest-dwarf spirit who causes mischief in the human world. Juan and Mudarríos were still working while Mudacerros was alone in the camp tending to the fire and cooking supper.

From *¡Teatro! Hispanic Plays for Young People*. Copyright © 1996. Teacher Ideas Press. (800) 237-6124.

(Mudacerros enters, singing to himself. As he is singing, the Duende enters, approaching Mudacerros to watch him.)

Mudacerros:	Mudacerros, Mudacerros All the work you did today Never was there such a man They should give you twice the pay!
The Duende:	*(Making fun of Mudacerros.)* Mudacerros, Mudacerros Are you sure you're not crazy With the little work you did today I know you're very lazy!
Mudacerros:	*(Turning around and confronting the Duende.)* Who are you to talk to me in that way? Do you know who you're talking to?
The Duende:	Mudacerros. Molehill mover?
Mudacerros:	I'll teach you respect! *(He reaches to strike at the Duende, but the Duende is too fast, and he dodges the blow.)* So you think you are fast, eh. Well soon you will be begging for my mercy. *(He attempts another blow and, as he chases the Duende, the Duende trips Mudacerros.)* That is the end of my kindness. Now you will pay with your life. *(As he lunges at the Duende, the Duende trips him again and, with devilish laughter, the Duende beats Mudacerros on the head, steals the pan with the food, and runs off.)*

(As the Duende exits, Juan and Mudarríos enter, running.)

Juan:	Mudacerros. What happened? We heard you yelling.
Mudacerros:	A horrible little man attacked me. He beat me up and stole our supper.
Mudarríos:	*(Laughing.)* A little man beat up the mighty Mountain Mover! I wish I could have seen that.
Mudacerros:	He was no ordinary little man. I'm sure he was a forest *Duende*. They have magical powers that allow them to cause mischief in the world.
Juan:	Why would they be here?
Mudarríos:	Their underground caverns are nearby. It is impossible to find them, but I have heard that they keep Princesses captive in those caverns.
Mudacerros:	Guarded by giants!
Mudarríos:	Well tomorrow I will cook the supper. I know the ways of *Duendes*, and that *Duende* will not get our food a second time.

(All exit.)

From ¡*Teatro! Hispanic Plays for Young People*. Copyright © 1996. Teacher Ideas Press. (800) 237-6124.

| The Narrator: | The next night. |

(*Mudarríos enters with another pan of food. He is suspiciously looking around. He places the pan down and begins to sing nervously to himself. As he sings, the Duende enters and makes fun of Mudarríos with a song of his own.*)

Mudarríos:	The night is very cold The *Duende* had better not be so bold Mudarríos, powerful man Will catch that *Duende* if he can.
The Duende:	Mudarríos, Mudarríos The *Duende* is too smart Scared and powerless man There is no way you can.
Mudarríos:	Duende! Now you will pay! (*He lunges at the Duende, but the Duende is too fast, and he escapes the blow. Mudarríos lunges at him again, and the Duende trips Mudarríos and begins to beat him on the head. Then, once again, he steals the pan of food and runs off.*)

(*As the Duende exits, Juan and Mudacerros enter, running.*)

Mudacerros:	What happened? Did you catch him?
Mudarríos:	He was too fast, the tricky little devil!
Juan:	And now we have to go another night without food. Tomorrow I will wait and I will catch that *Duende*!

(*All exit.*)

| The Narrator: | The next night. |

(*Juan enters and places the pan of food on the ground. He then circles the pan, singing to himself. As he sings, the Duende enters and makes fun of Juan.*)

| Juan: | Little man, little man
I dare you to show you face
If there is any way I can
You will never leave this place. |
| The Duende: | Two much better than you
Have tried and tried they said
And you have no clue
Before I beat you round the head. |

From *¡Teatro! Hispanic Plays for Young People.* Copyright © 1996. Teacher Ideas Press. (800) 237-6124.

(The Duende runs by Juan and tries to hit him on the head, but Juan is too fast and he catches the Duende by the corner of his shirt. The Duende runs off screaming, with Juan holding onto his shirt. As they exit, Mudarríos and Mudacerros enter, running.)

Mudarríos:	Juan! Where are you!
Mudacerros:	I heard his yelling. Look, the pan of food is still here. Oh no, the *Duende* carried off Juan this time!

(Juan enters carrying the Duende's shirt.)

Juan:	I caught him. Here is his shirt.
Mudarríos:	But where is the *Duende*?
Juan:	I saw him go into a hole in the ground. It must be the opening to their underground caverns.
Mudacerros:	There are stolen treasures under there. We could be rich. Show us the place.
Juan:	I looked down the hole. It is too deep. We will have to lower one of us down with a rope.
Mudarríos:	Well let's go get a rope!

(They grab the pan of food and exit.)

Scene 4: In the Duende's cavern.

The Narrator:	Mudarríos and Mudacerros lowered Juan down into the cave. At the bottom of the cave, Juan did find the treasures Mudacerros had talked about. He also discovered a room that held three captive Princesses. The first Princess was guarded by a giant, the second by a tiger, and the third by a serpent. Each tried to stop Juan, but his strength was too much for all of them. Juan was able to defeat all three and release the Princesses from their captivity.

(Juan and the three Princesses enter and stay at one side of the stage. Mudarríos and Mudacerros enter and stay at the other side of the stage.)

Juan:	You are safe now. We must return to the mouth of the cavern, and my two friends will be able to lift you out with a rope.
Princess #1:	Thank you for rescuing us. Our father is the King and he will reward you handsomely.
Princess #2:	No one has ever found the *Duende*'s caverns. We have waited and waited to be rescued. The *Duende* took care of us, but he would not let us leave.

From *¡Teatro! Hispanic Plays for Young People*. Copyright © 1996. Teacher Ideas Press. (800) 237-6124.

Princess #3:	(*Giving Juan two gems.*) Here are two gems from my crown. I give them to you to thank you for rescuing us.
Juan:	We better leave. The *Duende* will return any minute. My friends will pull you up with the rope. Then we can take you safely back to your castle. (*He calls up to Mudarríos and Mudacerros.*) Throw down the rope. The Princesses are ready to come up.
Mudacerros:	He must have rescued the Princesses. The King will reward handsomely whoever brings them back.
Mudarríos:	There is indeed a handsome reward here.
Mudacerros:	A reward split in two makes larger shares than a reward split in three.
Mudarríos:	Perhaps you are right. We were together long before he joined us.
Mudacerros:	This is our one chance to make our fortune.
Mudarríos:	You are right. Two parts are greater than three parts.

(*As the narrator speaks, the actors mime the action.*)

The Narrator:	Mudarríos and Mudacerros threw down the rope. Juan helped the three Princesses climb up the rope to their freedom. When the last Princess had climbed the rope, Mudarríos and Mudacerros pulled up the rope, leaving Juan stranded at the bottom.
Juan:	Hey, throw down the rope! Get me out of here!
Princess #3:	(*To Mudarríos.*) Aren't you going to help him?
Mudacerros:	No. We made an agreement that he would stay down and explore the caverns more, and we'll come back for him later.

(*Mudarríos, Mudacerros, and the three Princesses exit. As Juan is yelling
for help, the Duende enters.*)

Juan:	Help! Mudarríos, throw down the rope. Mudacerros, bring me up. Help!
The Duende:	What are you doing in my caverns? And where are the Princesses? Did you see where the treasures are hidden?

(*The Duende begins to hit Juan, but Juan is too strong for the Duende. He
picks up the Duende and holds him in the air.*)

Juan:	*Duende*, you better show me the way out of this cavern, or you will never leave it again yourself!
The Duende:	Put me down!
Juan:	*Duende*, this is your last chance! Show me the way out of this cavern!

From *¡Teatro! Hispanic Plays for Young People*. Copyright © 1996. Teacher Ideas Press. (800) 237-6124.

The Duende: | All right, already. Ouch, you're hurting my neck. The path out begins right over there. Ouch! Not so hard. Ouch.

(*Juan and the Duende exit, with the Duende complaining all the way.*)

Scene 5: The King's castle.

(*The King, the Queen, the three Princesses, Mudarríos, and Mudacerros enter.*)

The King: | I wish to reward you two for rescuing my daughters.

The Queen: | The whole kingdom owes you its gratitude. The Princesses are most beloved throughout the kingdom. You have brought joy back to our land.

The King: | The Princesses have told me there was a third man, a man who actually rescued them from the caverns.

Mudarríos: | No, they are mistaken. They were so scared and it was so dark in the caves that they imagined a third man. There was just myself and my friend.

(*As Mudarríos says these words, Juan enters.*)

Juan: | Your Majesty, those words are a lie!

The King: | Who are you who so rudely bursts into the King's chambers. Guards!

Princess #1: | Father, this is the man who rescued us.

Princess #2: | It is him. They said you were dead.

Mudarríos: | Your Majesty, this man is an impostor.

Mudacerros: | It was dark in the caves, and your daughters were suffering from their captivity. They could not see clearly enough to identify the man. This man is not our partner.

Mudarríos: | He is a thief trying to gain our reward.

Juan: | Please, your Majesty, may I speak?

Princess #3: | Let him speak, father.

The King: | You may speak.

Juan: | Your Majesty, examine closely the crown of your third daughter. It is missing two gem stones. Here are the stones your daughter gave me when we were in the caverns as I was rescuing them.

(*The King takes the crown of Princess #3. He examines it along with the two gems Juan hands him. He returns the crown to his daughter, and he returns the gems to Juan.*)

From *¡Teatro! Hispanic Plays for Young People*. Copyright © 1996. Teacher Ideas Press. (800) 237-6124.

The King: | Guards! (*Gesturing to Mudarríos and Mudacerros.*) Throw these two men into the dungeon.

(*The King's guards enter and carry off Mudarríos and Mudacerros.*)

The King: | (*Addressing Juan.*) And you, good sir. Join us in a celebration of the rescue of the Princesses. And know that those two gems you hold are but the first of many you shall receive as your reward for rescuing the Princesses.

(*All exit.*)

From ¡*Teatro! Hispanic Plays for Young People*. Copyright © 1996. Teacher Ideas Press. (800) 237-6124.

La Estrella de Oro
The Gold Star

Introduction

La Estrella de Oro, The Gold Star, is often called "The Hispanic Cinderella." It is a folktale based upon the well-known European story of the mistreated young girl who is befriended by a magical guardian. Of course, it ends with the marriage to a prince and the traditional "happily ever after."

This version contains many story elements that mark its adaptation to the Hispanic culture. In Hispanic versions, the magical guardian who befriends the young girl has been depicted most commonly in one of three ways: 1) as either the Virgin Mary herself; 2) as *La Viejita de La Buena Suerte*, the Little Old Woman of Good Luck, a magical godmother-like character; or 3) as a prince in an enchanted form, usually a bird. Another Hispanic story element is the washing of the *tripitas*, intestines, which was a common activity for a rural, self-sufficient people who had the practice of using all parts of the animal for food.

Staging

This story belongs to the category of magic and transformation tales. The most challenging staging problems are the gold star, the green horn, and the donkey ears. It is best to be straightforward about these magical transformations. In the script the characters each exit the stage and re-enter magically transformed. Their exits provide time to put on the star, horn, and donkey ears off-stage.

The character of the Virgin Mary can be changed to a nonreligious figure. This Hispanic version of this story type often contains the Virgin Mary as a defining characteristic. But if your situation requires a nonreligious character, the simple solution is to make this character *La Viejita de La Buena Suerte*, the Little Old Woman of Good Luck, a character much in line with the Fairy Godmother of the traditional European version. A few easy adjustments in the text will accomplish this change.

Props

Ears of corn	A bag of *tripitas*	Donkey ears
An earthen jar	A gold star	A green horn
A linen bag filled with white feathers	Pastries	
	Sparkling, glitter confetti for bird's tears	

Costumes

See figures 1, 2, 4, 6, and 8 in the introduction to this book. The birds are actors in costumes.

Cast of Characters

The Narrator	Stepsister #1	Birds
Estrellita, Little Star	Stepsister #2	The Prince
The Father	The Virgin Mary	The Cat
The Stepmother		

Scene 1: At the farm of Estrellita.

The Narrator:	*La Estrella de Oro*, The Gold Star, is the magical story of a mistreated young woman who is befriended by a kind and loving guardian. At the beginning of our story, the young woman Estrellita, which means Little Star, is consoling her father.

(Estrellita and the Father enter. They sit and begin husking corn.)

Estrellita:	Papa, the *elote* this year is fat and juicy.
The Father:	It has been a good year for *elote*. The sun was hot, the skies gave us plenty of water. And the ground is good.
Estrellita:	Don't forget the most important part. You're the best farmer in the whole valley.
The Father:	I was just blessed by the Lord this year.
Estrellita:	*(Holding up an ear of corn.)* The best in the whole world!
The Father:	Estrellita, don't get so carried away. Next year could be a year of drought, and then where will we be?
Estrellita:	What are we going to do with all this corn?
The Father:	Most of it will go to market, and we will keep enough for our own needs.
Estrellita:	I remember how Mama used to roast the *elote*. It was so delicious dipped in butter and salted. She was a wonderful cook!
The Father:	*(With a sadness in his voice.)* She was a wonderful woman.
Estrellita:	Papa, it breaks my heart to see you so sad and lonely.
The Father:	Ever since your mother died, it has not been easy for me to have the happy ways we shared when your mother was alive. Even the work of the farm is not enough to help me out of my sadness. The only joy in my life now is you, Estrellita, my little golden star.
Estrellita:	Papa, it is time for you to get married again.
The Father:	There is no one for me to marry. And there will never be another woman to replace your mother.
Estrellita:	I know that. I'm not trying to replace Mama. I just know how lonely you are, and perhaps two lonely people could come together for companionship and find a new happiness together.
The Father:	What do you mean "two lonely people"?

From *¡Teatro! Hispanic Plays for Young People.* Copyright © 1996. Teacher Ideas Press. (800) 237-6124.

Estrellita:	You know. Two lonely people. Two people who have lost their spouses and are . . . well, you know . . . lonely.
The Father:	Do you have any certain "two lonely people" in mind?
Estrellita:	(*Excitedly.*) Well, Papa, the widow who lives in the village, she is always really nice to me. Whenever I walk by her house, she invites me in for *biscochitos* or *arroz con leche.* She is always so nice to me. Her husband died several years ago, and she is always telling me how much she would like to get married again.
The Father:	I know the family you are talking about. I'm sure she is a nice woman, but that is not enough reason for me to marry her. First, she would have to want a husband. Then, we aren't even sure I am the man she would want. No, Estrellita, your idea is coming from a good place in your heart, but it is not the best idea for me.
Estrellita:	She even has two daughters, and we could be three wonderful sisters.
The Father:	Estrellita, who is the lonely one here?
Estrellita:	(*Frustrated.*) Papa, you're not even giving it a chance. Who knows? She is probably just as lonely as you. And you are still a handsome man. And with our farm, you have a lot to offer a woman. And her two daughters could use a father again. Papa, there are a lot of reasons it could work!
The Father:	Except the main one. I'm not looking for a new wife.
Estrellita:	Papa, it could make you happy again instead of sad all the time. (*She begins to cry.*)
The Father:	Estrellita, please don't cry. Ever since your mother died, I have tried to make a happy home for us. But I have been so consumed by my own sadness that I didn't notice how sad you have been. Just like those two daughters could use a father again, you could use a mother again. If this is something that will make you happy again, then I will give it a try. This Sunday after church, we will pay a visit to the widow and her two daughters and see what happens.
Estrellita:	Oh Papa, I just know we will be happy again!

(*They exit.*)

Scene 2: A while later.

The Narrator:	A few months later, the farmer did marry the widow. He loved Estrellita so much that he would do anything to try and bring happiness back into her life. At first, the widow and her two daughters were agreeable, and the

From ¡*Teatro! Hispanic Plays for Young People.* Copyright © 1996. Teacher Ideas Press. (800) 237-6124.

first few months of the new family's life were filled with an easy joy. But soon the widow's true nature began to surface. She began to mistreat Estrellita and favor her own two daughters. The father spent long hours working in the fields, and he often was not around to witness the woman's cruelty to Estrellita.

(*The Stepmother and Stepsisters enter. During this scene, the Stepsisters primp and tend to their clothes.*)

The Stepmother:	Estrellita! Come here.
Estrellita:	Yes, I'm here. I was—
The Stepmother:	What took you so long! I called and called and still no Estrellita. What were you doing?
Estrellita:	You told me to clean the kitchen floor, and I was busy getting water to mop the floor. I didn't hear you.
Stepsister #1:	Estrellita, I thought Mama told you to get me some clean clothes. I'm so hot and dirty I want to change dresses.
Stepsister #2:	Me too. Bring me the blue one with the lace and—
The Stepmother:	Now girls, I'm sure Estrellita will get to your clothes just as soon as she has finished the chores I have given her. Won't you, Estrellita?
Estrellita:	Yes, I will. But there is a lot to do. You told me—
Stepsister #1:	Mama! Estrellita isn't going to get me a clean dress!
Estrellita:	I will but first I—
Stepsister #2:	Mama! Make Estrellita get me a clean dress!
The Stepmother:	Estrellita, you should be finished with those chores by now. If you weren't so lazy, all those chores would be done.
Estrellita:	If those two lazy girls would help instead of spending the day—
Stepsisters:	Mama! Estrellita called us lazy!
The Stepmother:	Estrellita apologize to your sisters at once.
Estrellita:	But—
The Stepmother:	Don't talk back to me. You are the rudest child. Absolutely no manners at all. Your father has done the worst job of raising you.
Estrellita:	Don't talk about my father that way!
The Stepmother:	Estrellita, go to your room! There will be no supper for you tonight.

From *¡Teatro! Hispanic Plays for Young People*. Copyright © 1996. Teacher Ideas Press. (800) 237-6124.

Stepsisters:	But who will get our dresses now? (*They start crying.*)
The Stepmother:	Estrellita! Now look what you have done. You have made your two sisters cry. Now their beautiful skin will have tear stains on it. (*She examines the faces of her two daughters.*) There is only one way they will be able to wash away these stains. You must go into the forest and bring back a jug filled with bird tears. Only the tears of birds are pure enough to wash the skin of my daughters.
Estrellita:	But that is an impossible task. I'll never be able to fill a jar with bird tears.
The Stepmother:	Then don't come back until you do.
Estrellita:	My father will ask where I am.
The Stepmother:	Then we will just tell him the truth. That you ran away. It will break his heart to know that it was you who brought such unhappiness to his new family.
Estrellita:	I am the cause of all this unhappiness. Now my father does nothing but work all the time and we are no happier than we were before.
The Stepmother:	Then you better do what I say, or I'll have to tell your father what has happened.

(*The two Stepsisters begin to cry again, and the Stepmother consoles them.*)

Estrellita:	I will do what you ask.
The Stepmother:	That's a good girl. And while you're in the forest, bring back a bag filled with bird feathers. They are the only fillings soft enough for my daughters' pillows. They've had such a terrible day, I want them to sleep as peacefully as possible tonight. Now go. Get started.

(*The Stepmother and Stepsisters exit, talking about how horrible Estrellita is. Estrellita exits, walking out sadly.*)

Scene 3: In the forest.

The Narrator:	And so Estrellita went into the forest on her impossible tasks. As she wandered through the forest, she sang to cheer herself up. To her surprise, she was answered by a beautiful voice.

(*Estrellita enters, carrying an earthen jar and a linen bag. She searches and searches the sky but soon gives up. She begins to talk to herself.*)

Estrellita:	Why did I ever make my family so unhappy? This is all my fault. My father and I are more unhappy than we were before. I know my father didn't want to marry the widow, but he did it hoping it would make me happy again. But now look what has happened. I wish there was a way I could make

From ¡*Teatro! Hispanic Plays for Young People.* Copyright © 1996. Teacher Ideas Press. (800) 237-6124.

everything return to how it was before. But that will never happen. I wish my mother was still here. She would know what to tell me. She always said that, if I was in trouble, I could turn to the Blessed Mother and everything would be better. (*She begins to sing to herself.*)

In the early morning sun
I try to find happiness for the day
For each and everyone
Happiness in every single way.
There can never be a day so dark
That I will never find
A chance to make my mark
And bring peace to every mind.

(*A beautiful voice is heard singing off-stage.*)

The Virgin Mary:	(*From off-stage.*) Estrellita, little star. You are a heart as pure as gold A spirit that is ever true With all the powers that I hold I will send the birds of the air to help you.
Estrellita:	(*Looking around.*) Where is that voice coming from?

(*As Estrellita speaks, the Birds fly into the scene and drop downy white feathers on Estrellita. The also fly over the jar and drop their tears into it. As the birds fly off, Estrellita gathers up the feathers and puts them into the linen bag.*)

Estrellita:	(*Looking into the earthen jar.*) Filled with bird's tears! Oh Blessed Mother, thank you! (*She exits.*)

Scene 4: At the farm of Estrellita.

The Narrator:	Estrellita returned home with the bird tears and the downy feathers. Soon her father returned home. Her father was determined to provide for his new family in the best way possible, and this meant extra-long hours in the field working. Because of this, however, he was unaware of the stepmother's mistreatment of Estrellita. As he arrived, he brought a present for each of the girls.

(*The Stepmother and the Stepsisters enter.*)

Stepsister #1:	I thought Estrellita was supposed to bring back bird tears from the forest.
The Stepmother:	Don't be so stupid. She will never be able to get bird tears. That was just an excuse to get her lost in the forest. If she never comes back, that will be the best for us, my two lovely daughters.

From *¡Teatro! Hispanic Plays for Young People*. Copyright © 1996. Teacher Ideas Press. (800) 237-6124.

Stepsister #2:	But what about her father?
The Stepmother:	Oh he will be sad for sure, but he will get over it. After all, he has a new family now, and he has two daughters to replace that one.
Stepsister #1:	Mama, this was such a good idea of yours. All those afternoons of giving *biscochitos* to Estrellita sure paid off.
The Stepmother:	I told you I'd find you a new father and me a new husband. My plan has worked out beautifully up to now. There are just a couple more small details to work out, and soon all this will be ours.
Stepsister #2:	Shhh! Here he comes.

(*The Father enters.*)

The Father:	I'm home. (*Looking around.*) And where is my daughter Estrellita? She is always here to greet me.
The Stepmother:	Oh, I sent her do to an errand in the forest. I hope nothing has happened to her.
The Father:	What could happen?
The Stepmother:	Nothing I hope.
The Father:	She has been in the forest before. But not this late. I better go looking for her.
The Stepmother:	You just got home. Rest for a while. I just finished your favorite meal. *Calabacitas* and *arroz con pollo.*
The Father:	Chicken with rice. My favorite!
The Stepmother:	It is hot right now. We should eat while the food is hot. My two daughters have been waiting for you to come home for dinner. You don't want to disappoint them, do you?
The Father:	Estrellita will be home soon. She knows her way around the forest. Let's eat dinner.

(*Estrellita enters, filled with excitement.*)

Estrellita:	Papa! The most wonderful thing happened to me in the forest!
The Father:	Estrellita! Slow down. We were just sitting down for dinner. (*To the Stepmother.*) See, I told you she would be all right.
The Stepmother:	(*Looking at the Stepsisters and shrugging her shoulders.*) I was sure she would be all right. I didn't want anything to happen to my new beautiful daughter Estrellita.
Estrellita:	Papa, Mama sent me into the forest with this jar and bag—

From ¡*Teatro! Hispanic Plays for Young People.* Copyright © 1996. Teacher Ideas Press. (800) 237-6124.

The Stepmother:	(*Quickly grabbing the jar and bag from Estrellita.*) Just give those things to me, Estrellita. I'm sure your father isn't interested in every little errand I send you on.
Estrellita:	But I got the—
The Stepmother:	I'm sure you did. (*Giving the jar and bag to the Stepsisters. The Stepsisters look in them and look back at the Stepmother in amazement. The Stepmother grabs them back and looks inside them. She looks up in amazement and gives them back to the Stepsisters.*) Why, what a good little girl you are, Estrellita. You got just what I asked for. Tomorrow you will have to tell me just how you did it.
The Father:	Estrellita, what did you do that was so special?
Estrellita:	It wasn't me. That is what I've been trying to tell you.
The Stepmother:	(*Trying to get rid of her.*) Estrellita, dearest, your father has had a long, hard day. I'll tell him myself later. Let's let him eat now, and you girls can go to bed early tonight so he can have some peace and quiet.
The Father:	Before you go off, I have a special present for each of you girls.
Stepsister #2:	What is it! Let me have it!
Stepsister #1:	No, give me mine first!
The Stepmother:	Now girls. Remember your manners. Now, what is it you brought my daughters.
The Father:	And Estrellita, too.
The Stepmother:	Of course. Whenever I say "my daughters" nowadays I mean Estrellita too.
The Father:	(*Bringing Estrellita over to him.*) Remember the year the *elote* was the best ever? Well this year the crop was even better. All my hard work in the field has paid off. I've made so much money this year, I was able to buy each of you your own lamb. You will be able to raise the lamb and sell it at market, and you can keep whatever money you make off the sale.
Stepsister #1:	A lamb. I wanted a new dress.
Stepsister #2:	Raise a lamb. Yuk! They're too stinky.
The Father:	But when they are grown, you can sell them and the money will be yours.
The Stepmother:	Now girls, be thankful for your present. I'm sure Estrellita will be willing to help raise the lambs for you. Won't you, Estrellita?
Estrellita:	I guess so.

From *¡Teatro! Hispanic Plays for Young People.* Copyright © 1996. Teacher Ideas Press. (800) 237-6124.

The Father:	You're a good daughter, Estrellita. Your two new sisters have not been raised on a farm like you have, and I'm sure they appreciate that you will help them.
Estrellita:	If you say so, Papa.
The Stepmother:	My, look how late it's gotten. Time for bed for, everyone. Say goodnight to your father.
Stepsister #1:	Goodnight.
Stepsister #2:	Goodnight.
Estrellita:	(*Giving her father a big hug.*) Goodnight, Papa. I love you.
The Father:	Goodnight, *jita*. I love you, too.

(*All exit.*)

Scene 5: A few days later.

The Narrator:	A few days later, the stepmother told Estrellita something that would make the beginning of another adventure for Estrellita.

(*The Stepmother and Stepsisters enter. The Stepsisters are stuffing themselves with sweet pastries. They giggle throughout the scene.*)

The Stepmother:	Estrellita! Come here!
Estrellita:	(*Rushing in.*) You called? I came as fast as I could.
The Stepmother:	That's better. Have you finished making the beds?
Estrellita:	Almost.
The Stepmother:	Good. When you are done, I have another job for you. We have slaughtered your lamb and I want you to go to the river and wash the *tripitas*. We will use them to stuff and make *chorizo*.
Estrellita:	You killed my lamb? Why?
The Stepmother:	I told you. We had to get some *tripitas* to make sausage. Your lamb was the one we had to use. Now take those *tripitas* to the river and clean them. I want them clean, inside and out. And don't lose a single one of them. If you lose one, you will be sorry. Now get back to work. And have those *tripitas* back here by noon.

(*Estrellita exits.*)

Stepsisters:	(*Laughing as Estrellita exits.*) Sorry about your lamb.

(*The Stepmother and Stepsisters exit.*)

From *¡Teatro! Hispanic Plays for Young People.* Copyright © 1996. Teacher Ideas Press. (800) 237-6124.

Scene 6: At the river.

*(Estrellita enters. She mimes the action in the scene. As the scene begins,
she is at the river washing the tripitas.)*

The Narrator:	Estrellita, brokenhearted about her lamb, went to the river to wash the *tripitas.* She tried not to think about her little lamb, and tried to remember better days when her mother was alive and her family was together and happy.
Estrellita:	I know that some day my Papa and I will be happy together. We will live in a big castle on top of the highest mountain. And he will never have to work in the field again. And I will be married to a prince . . . *(She begins to cry.)* My poor little lamb. I loved it so. Now it is as sad as I am. I wonder if we will ever be happy again. Oh no! The river has carried away the *tripitas*! I should have been more careful. I knew the water was too high and too fast. Now my stepmother will have every reason to punish me. I'll never be able to get the *tripitas* back. *(Suddenly she hears the familiar voice, singing.)*

(A beautiful voice of the Virgin Mary is heard singing off-stage.)

The Virgin Mary:	Do not be afraid my dearest child Do not run and try to hide You are not alone here in the wild I am always here by your side.
Estrellita:	Is that you again, Blessed Mother?

(The Virgin Mary enters.)

The Virgin Mary:	I am always by your side. Here are your *tripitas.*
Estrellita:	The *tripitas*! You saved them. Thank you!
The Virgin Mary:	Do not lose hope, Estrellita. One day all your dreams will come true. Your own good heart will make them so.
Estrellita:	You were the one who sent me the bird's tears and feathers. And now you've saved me again.
The Virgin Mary:	Your own good spirit is what saves you.
Estrellita:	My mother always said you would be there for me.
The Virgin Mary:	*(She touches Estrellita on the head.)* When you return, you will have a gift from me. A gift that will show your good spirit to all who see you. It will be the spirit of Estrellita, Little Star.*(She exits.)*
Estrellita:	Thank you, Blessed Mother. *(She exits.)*

From *¡Teatro! Hispanic Plays for Young People.* Copyright © 1996. Teacher Ideas Press. (800) 237-6124.

Scene 7: At the farm.

(*The Stepmother and Stepsisters enter.*)

The Stepmother:	Estrellita! Are you back yet? Where is that Estrellita?
Stepsister #1:	She needs to be punished, Mama.
Stepsister #2:	She should be back by now. I bet she didn't even wash the *tripitas*.
The Stepmother:	Don't worry. She will be punished.

(*Estrellita enters. She is carrying the bag of* tripitas. *On her forehead is a gold star. When the Stepmother and Stepsister see it, they gasp.*)

Estrellita:	I'm back, and the *tripitas* are all clean. Here they are.
Stepsisters:	Estrellita!
The Stepmother:	Estrellita! Where have you been?
Estrellita:	Down at the river. Washing the *tripitas*.
The Stepmother:	What happened to you?
Estrellita:	Nothing. I hurried right back because I knew you needed the *tripitas*.
Stepsister #2:	Your forehead. It's shining.
Stepsister #1:	Really bright.
The Stepmother:	There's a golden star on your forehead.
Estrellita:	A golden star!

(*The Stepsisters reach forward to touch the star, but Estrellita pulls back before they can touch it.*)

The Stepmother:	(*Angrily.*) Where did you get that star? Take it off at once!
Estrellita:	(*Estrellita tries to remove the star, but it won't come off.*) I can't take it off. It's stuck.
The Stepmother:	Here, let me take it off. (*She tries, but it won't come off.*)
Stepsister #1:	Mama, I want a star on my forehead!
Stepsister #2:	Mama, now she is more beautiful than us! I want a star on my forehead!
Stepsisters:	We want a star on our forehead! We want a star—
The Stepmother:	Quiet, you two! Now, Estrellita, tell me how you got the star on your forehead.

From ¡*Teatro! Hispanic Plays for Young People.* Copyright © 1996. Teacher Ideas Press. (800) 237-6124.

Estrellita:	I didn't know I was getting a star on my forehead. The Blessed Mother just said I would have a gift.
Stepsisters:	We want stars on our foreheads!
The Stepmother:	I said quiet, you two!
Stepsister #1:	Estrellita always gets everything!
The Stepmother:	Where were you when you saw the Blessed Mother?
Estrellita:	I was down by the river washing the *tripitas*. I dropped them and they started going down the river, and the Blessed Mother saved them for me. Then she said she would give me a gift, and I would have it when I got back home. I didn't know it was going to be a gold star.
Stepsisters:	We want a gold star too! Mama, get us a gold star like Estrellita has.
The Stepmother:	Estrellita, go outside. Leave me alone. I have to think about things.

(*Estrellita exits.*)

Stepsister #1:	You have a plan, don't you, Mama?
The Stepmother:	Let me think. Let me think . . . Yes, I have a wonderful plan. My beautiful daughters, get ready. You are going down to the river.
Stepsister #1:	The river! It's full of snakes.
Stepsister #2:	And bugs! I hate the river!
The Stepmother:	(*Angrily.*) Well you're both going! Now get started, and do as I say!

(*The Stepmother and Stepsisters exit, arguing.*)

Scene 8: At the river.

(*The Stepsisters enter, carrying a bag of* tripitas.)

Stepsister #1:	Is this the river?
Stepsister #2:	I think so. I've never been down here.
Stepsister #1:	Do you remember what to do?
Stepsister #2:	Sure I do. Do you? Do you think this will really work?
Stepsister #1:	Mama said it would. Now go ahead.
Stepsister #2:	What if it doesn't work?
Stepsister #1:	It's going to work. Now throw the bag.

From ¡*Teatro! Hispanic Plays for Young People.* Copyright © 1996. Teacher Ideas Press. (800) 237-6124.

Stepsister #2:	No you. I'm afraid.
Stepsister #1:	Well here goes. (*She throws the* tripitas *into the river.*)
Stepsister #2:	They are going down the river, but nothing is happening.
Stepsister #1:	We have to ask for help. Just like Estrellita told us.
Stepsister #2:	(*In a halting, feeble manner.*) Help! Help!
Stepsister #1:	Look, here comes someone. She has the bag of *tripitas.*

(*The Virgin Mary enters, carrying the bag of* tripitas.)

The Virgin Mary:	I have returned your bag.
Stepsister #2:	I don't want that stupid bag! Give me my star. You gave Estrellita one, and I want one too.
Stepsister #1:	A gold one!
The Virgin Mary:	The golden star was Estrellita's gift because of her good spirit.
Stepsister #2:	My spirit is good, too. Give me my star.
Stepsister #1:	If you don't give me my star, I'm going to tell my Mama.
Stepsister #2:	Then I'll get my star.
The Virgin Mary:	(*She touches both of them on the head.*) When you return, you will have your gift. The gift will show your true spirit to all who see you. (*She exits.*)
Stepsisters:	I have my gold star. I have my gold star. (*They exit.*)

Scene 9: At the farm.

(*Estrellita and the Stepmother enter.*)

The Stepmother:	Those girls should be back by now. Are you sure you told me exactly how it happened?
Estrellita:	Everything. Exactly as it happened.
The Stepmother:	Well it better work for those girls. Their hearts will be broken if you are the only one with a gold star on your forehead.
Estrellita:	I didn't ask for the star. The Blessed Mother gave it to me.

(*The Stepsisters enter. One has a green horn on her forehead, and the other has donkey ears. They are unaware of what is on their heads, and they are primping as if they are beautiful. The Stepmother is aghast.*)

From ¡*Teatro! Hispanic Plays for Young People.* Copyright © 1996. Teacher Ideas Press. (800) 237-6124.

Stepsister #1:	Mama, we saw the woman. It was just like Estrellita said it would be.
Stepsister #2:	I don't think she really wanted to give us the gold stars, but we talked her into it.
Stepsister #1:	Isn't it beautiful?
Stepsister #2:	I think mine is more beautiful. More golden.
Stepsister #1:	Mine shines more . . .
The Stepmother:	Oh no! This is horrible.
Stepsister #1:	What? What is wrong?
Stepsister #2:	Is my star falling off?
Estrellita:	Sisters, I am so sorry. I'm so sorry.
Stepsister #1:	What is wrong? Tell me.
The Stepmother:	Just look at each other.

(*For the first time, the Stepsisters look at each other.*)

Stepsister #1:	You have donkey ears.
Stepsister #2:	You have a green horn.
Stepsisters:	Oh no! Estrellita, how did this happen?
Estrellita:	I don't know.
The Stepmother:	Let me try to take them off.

(*The Stepmother and Stepsisters all try to take off the donkey ears and green horn. But they do not come off.*)

Stepsister #1:	I'm ugly.
Stepsister #2:	I'm more ugly
The Stepmother:	Estrellita, this is your fault. You will pay for this!

(*All exit.*)

Scene 10: At the farm.

The Narrator:	No matter how hard they tried, the green horn and the donkey ears wouldn't come off. And Estrellita's golden star just seemed to glow brighter and brighter. Every day, Estrellita went to church to pray for the green horn and donkey ears to fall off her stepsisters' heads. She didn't actually go

From *¡Teatro! Hispanic Plays for Young People.* Copyright © 1996. Teacher Ideas Press. (800) 237-6124.

into the church, because her golden star shined too brightly and it distracted everybody. So she just stood outside the church, looking in the window. One day, the Prince was traveling through the village and he stopped and came to the church. While he was in the church, he noticed a bright light shining through the church window. The more he looked, the brighter the light became. Finally, he had to see the source of the light. When he looked out the window, he saw that it was the golden star shining on Estrellita's forehead. When he saw her, he saw her great beauty and, through the gold star, he also saw her good spirit. He immediately fell in love with her. When Estrellita saw him looking at her, she became afraid and ran back home. The Prince rushed out of the church, but Estrellita was gone. When he couldn't find her, the Prince ordered a search of all the farmhouses in the area.

(*The Stepmother, Stepsisters, and the Cat enter. The Cat curls up at the edge of the stage.*)

Stepsister #1:	Mama, did you hear? The Prince is searching all the farmhouses looking for the woman he is in love with. When he finds her, he is going to make her his Queen.
Stepsister #2:	He's looking for a woman with a gold star on her head. That's Estrellita.
The Stepmother:	Well, he won't find her here. I locked her up in the cellar.
Stepsister #1:	Mama, here comes the Prince.

(*The Prince enters. The Stepmother and Stepsisters bow.*)

The Stepmother:	Welcome. We hope you find what you are looking for here.
The Prince:	So do I. I have searched all the farms in the valley, and I have not found the woman I am looking for.
The Stepmother:	That is because you have not yet met my daughters.
The Prince:	Please give me the honor of meeting them now.
The Stepmother:	This is my second, my youngest daughter.

(*As Stepsister #2 comes forward and bows, the Prince reaches out and touches the donkey ears.*)

The Prince:	(*As kindly as possible.*) I am sorry, but I am not looking for a woman with donkey ears.

(*Stepsister #2 bursts out crying.*)

The Stepmother:	Of course you're not. How foolish of me. Here is my first, my oldest daughter.

From *¡Teatro! Hispanic Plays for Young People.* Copyright © 1996. Teacher Ideas Press. (800) 237-6124.

(Stepsister #1 comes forward and bows to the Prince. As she bows, the Prince reaches out and touches the green horn.)

The Prince:	(*As kindly as possible.*) I wasn't looking for a woman with a green horn, either. I was actually looking for a woman with a shining gold star. Thank you, but I must be going.
The Stepmother:	(*Grabbing the Prince by the arm before he can leave.*) But you don't realize. This horn shines when you look at it from the side. (*She pulls the Prince around from side to side of Stepsister #1.*) See, just stand there and look.
The Prince:	I don't see it shining.
The Stepmother:	Oh silly me. It's the other side. See, look right here. When the light hits it just right, it sparkles.
The Prince:	It still isn't shining.
The Stepmother:	(*Getting desperate.*) It has to shine. It just has to. (*Rubbing the horn.*) Let me polish it.
The Prince:	I really must be going.
The Stepmother:	(*Pulling at the Prince's arm.*) Please don't. It shines. It shines!
The Cat:	Estrellita is in the cellar. The Little Star you seek is in the cellar.

(The Stepsisters shriek.)

The Prince:	Who said that?
The Stepmother:	No one. No one. You really must be going.
The Cat:	Estrellita, the Little Star, the Golden Star, is in the cellar.
The Prince:	(*Not believing what he is hearing.*) The cat is talking. Where did you get a talking cat?
The Stepmother:	The cat's not talking. It's just my daughter making funny noises. Good-bye now. (*She tries to push the Prince out the door.*)
The Cat:	Turn around. Turn around. Here is Estrellita.

(The Prince stops and turns around. When he does, Estrellita enters. The Prince walks over to Estrellita and stands looking at her. He reaches out and touches the gold star. Then he kneels on one knee and kisses her hand. The Stepmother and Stepsisters cry.)

The Narrator:	And so ends the story of Estrellita, *La Estrella de Oro*, The Gold Star. Of course the Prince made her his Queen, and she and her father now do live in a castle on top of the highest mountain. And her stepmother and stepsisters? Well, they are the best servants the castle ever had.

From *¡Teatro! Hispanic Plays for Young People*. Copyright © 1996. Teacher Ideas Press. (800) 237-6124.

Part II
Animal Fables

The Littlest Ant

Introduction

According to the classification categories of folktales, this story is a cumulative tale. As the story develops, repeated phrases are connected together to become a rhythmic chant describing the action of the story. At the end of the story all the phrases together form one long summary of the dramatic elements of the story.

This tale, *The Littlest Ant,* is a well-known and all-time favorite Hispanic folktale. Several versions of it exist, and they all vary in the endings and in the way the little ant solves its problems. They also vary in the numbers and types of characters in the story and the way they affect one another. This version contains most of the primary characters and follows the traditional version closely.

Staging

This is a wonderful student's participation story. The structure of the play is based more on mime movement than dialogue. The most effective way to prepare students to perform this play is to conduct improvisational games with them in which they create the movements of the characters of the play.

Also, there is the possibility of multiple casting of most of the parts. For example, the wind could be played by several students instead of just one. The play also allows for the possibility of choral dialogue. In the instance of the wind given previously, all the students playing the wind could speak the wind's dialogue together. The repeated phrase refrain, which is the defining characteristic of this type of story, also gives the opportunity for choral dialogue with more than one student speaking the refrain together. Every time the little ant says one of the refrains, a chorus of voices can join it.

A third playful activity is to have the students invent interesting voices for each of the characters.

Props

A large snowflake (see fig. 6 in the introduction to this book).

Costumes

See figure 6 in the introduction to this book.

Cast of Characters

The Narrator	The Cloud	The Cat
The Littlest Ant, Hormiguita	The Wind	The Dog
Father Ant	The Wall	The Stick
Mother Ant	The Mouse	The Fire
The Sun	The Owl	The Water

Scene 1: At the anthill.

The Narrator:	Once there was a little baby ant. This ant loved to play outside and hardly ever came into the anthill when her parents called her. One day the ant learned a lesson that she would never forget.

(*Father Ant and Mother Ant enter.*)

Father Ant:	Now where is Hormiguita? I told her to stay close to the anthill in case we needed her help.
Mother Ant:	You know Hormiguita. She is probably outside playing.
Father Ant:	But ants aren't supposed to play. Our life is one of work, work, work. You can look at any anthill at any time and all you will see is ants working. Digging, carrying. Doing ant work.
Mother Ant:	I don't know what we are going to do with Hormiguita. The other ants are beginning to talk about her.
Father Ant:	What are they saying?
Mother Ant:	They are saying that we have done a terrible job of raising her.
Father Ant:	They are saying what! They should mind their own children better before they start talking about Hormiguita. (*Yelling.*) Hormiguita! You get in here this minute.

(*Hormiguita runs in.*)

Hormiguita:	What is it papa? I was outside playing.
Father Ant:	That is exactly what it is. Do you know what an ant's number-one job is?
Hormiguita:	Uh, not really papa.
Father Ant:	It's quite clear you don't. An ant's number-one job is work!
Hormiguita:	Oh no, not the work lecture again.
Father Ant:	Yes the work lecture again. It's time, way past time in fact, for you to start helping with the work in the anthill.
Hormiguita:	(*In a whining voice.*) Papa, work is so boring.
Mama Ant:	Hormiguita, your father is right. As an ant, you need to help with the work of the anthill. It isn't right that you don't help. All the other ants your age help with digging new tunnels and carrying food in from the field. It's not right that all you do is play.
Hormiguita:	Oh, all right. I'll start working.

From *¡Teatro! Hispanic Plays for Young People*. Copyright © 1996. Teacher Ideas Press. (800) 237-6124.

Father Ant:	That's what you said last time we had this talk, and here we are having it again.
Hormiguita:	I guess I really mean it this time.
Father Ant:	I hope so, because if you don't, there's going to be big trouble.
Hormiguita:	I said OKAY.
Mother Ant:	Good, because there is a big piece of food outside and you need to bring it in.
Hormiguita:	(*Still sulking.*) OKAY.
Father Ant:	We are going to help dig a new tunnel at the back end of the anthill. As soon as you've brought in the food, come find us and help with the digging.
Hormiguita:	OKAY.
Father Ant:	Now, I'm counting on you. Whatever you do, don't start playing and wander away from the anthill, because a big storm is coming.
Hormiguita:	OKAY.

(*All exit.*)

Scene 2: Outside the anthill.

The Narrator:	As soon as Hormiguita got outside, she forgot everything her parents had told her, and she began playing again. Before long, she had wandered away from the anthill into the forest.

(*Hormiguita enters—playing, chasing a blowing leaf.*)

Hormiguita:	Wheeee! I almost caught it that time. Chasing leaves is so much fun. A lot more fun that working . . . Oh my gosh, I forgot I was supposed to bring that food into the anthill. Now I'm going to really be in big trouble. I better get back before they find out I've been playing again. (*She turns and starts to go back, but she stops and looks around because she is lost.*) I've never been in this part of the forest before. Now let's see. I think the path is that way . . . no, it isn't that way it's this way . . . no . . . I hope I'm not lost.

(*As the Narrator speaks, Hormiguita mimes the action.*)

The Narrator:	Hormiguita tried to find the way back home, but she had wandered too deep into the forest and was lost. Also, she had not noticed that a winter storm was moving in. As she stopped to figure out what to do, a large snowflake floated down from the sky and landed on her. The snowflake was very heavy and it trapped Hormiguita. No matter how hard she tried, she could not budge the snowflake. Soon she tired of the struggle and just lay there trapped by the snowflake.

From ¡*Teatro! Hispanic Plays for Young People*. Copyright © 1996. Teacher Ideas Press. (800) 237-6124.

Hormiguita:	This is just great. First I forget to do my work. Then I get lost in the forest. And now I'm trapped under a giant snowflake. Help! Help! . . . No answer. I'm really thirsty, too. This snowflake is too frozen to drink. I'm going to die of thirst . . . *¡Agua! ¡Agua!* Someone bring me some water! . . . *¡Agua! ¡Agua!* . . . This makes me really mad. Snowflake, get off my leg so I can go home. Snowflake, I'm talking to you. Get off my leg so I can go home!
The Narrator:	Of course the snowflake was frozen and didn't budge. Then Hormiguita noticed the sun up in the sky looking down at her .

(*The Sun enters.*)

Hormiguita:	*Sol*, melt the snowflake until it gets off my leg, so I can go home.
The Narrator:	But the sun just looked down from the sky and did nothing.
Hormiguita:	*Sol*, I said melt the snowflake until it gets off my leg, so I can go home.
The Sun:	Well little ant. That's too much work. I don't think so.
Hormiguita:	That sun is too lazy and afraid of a little work.
The Narrator:	Then Hormiguita noticed a cloud in the sky.

(*The Cloud enters.*)

Hormiguita:	*Nube* in the sky, cover the sun, until the sun melts the snowflake, until the snowflake gets off my leg, so I can go home.
The Narrator:	But the cloud did nothing.
Hormiguita:	*Nube*, I said cover the sun, until the sun melts the snowflake, until the snowflake gets off my leg, so I can go home.
The Cloud:	Little ant, can't you see I'm playing. That's too much work right now. I don't think so.
Hormiguita:	All that cloud wants to do is play! Doesn't it know that you can't play all the time.
The Narrator:	Then Hormiguita noticed the wind.

(*The Wind enters.*)

Hormiguita:	Oh good, the wind will help me! *Viento*, please help me. Blow the cloud in the sky, until the cloud covers the sun, until the sun melts the snowflake, until the snowflake gets off my leg, so I can go home.
The Narrator:	But the wind was too busy blowing here and there and didn't even look at Hormiguita.

From *¡Teatro! Hispanic Plays for Young People.* Copyright © 1996. Teacher Ideas Press. (800) 237-6124.

Hormiguita:	*Viento*, I said blow the cloud in the sky, until the cloud covers the sun, until the sun melts the snowflake, until the snowflake gets off my leg, so I can go home.
The Wind:	That would be too much work, and I'm having too much fun now. I don't think so.
Hormiguita:	I'm never going to get out of here . . . *¡Agua! ¡Agua!* I'm thirsty. Someone help me! . . . The sun, the cloud, and the wind are all too lazy to help me.

(*The Wall enters.*)

Hormiguita:	But there is a wall over there. It's all by itself, but it used to be part of a house here in the forest. The people probably moved, and all that's left of the house is that old, broken-down wall. That wall will help me. *Pared*, help me. Can you feel the wind just blowing around every which way? Well, it's just playing. It isn't even doing something useful. *Pared*, block the wind, until the wind blows the cloud in the sky, until the cloud covers the sun, until the sun melts the snowflake, until the snowflake gets off my leg, so I can go home . . . The wall isn't even moving. It's just standing there! Wall, I said block the wind, until the wind blows the cloud in the sky, until the cloud covers the sun, until the sun melts the snowflake, until the snowflake gets off my leg, so I can go home.
The Wall:	(*In a slow, heavy voice.*) I'm too old and tired. That would be too much work. I hate work. I don't think so.
The Narrator:	Hormiguita was getting very discouraged. No one wanted to work to help her. Just when she was giving up hope, a little mouse scurried by.

(*The Mouse enters, running playfully.*)

Hormiguita:	*Ratón, ratón*, over here. I'm trapped under this snowflake and no one will help me. You're the only one who can help me. Go over and gnaw at the wall, until the wall blocks the wind, until the wind blows the cloud in the sky, until the cloud covers the sun, until the sun melts the snowflake, until the snowflake gets off my leg, so I can go home.
The Mouse:	(*In a high, squeaky voice.*) Who me? I'm too small.
Hormiguita:	No you're not. Mice gnaw through walls in houses all the time, looking for food!
The Mouse:	Well, the truth is, I'm not hungry right now, and that would be too much work. I don't think so.
Hormiguita:	*Ratón*, don't be so lazy. It's not too much work.
The Mouse:	Yes it is. And besides, work is boring.

From *¡Teatro! Hispanic Plays for Young People.* Copyright © 1996. Teacher Ideas Press. (800) 237-6124.

Hormiguita:	Mouse, you'll be sorry, because I just saw a big owl fly by. *¡Tecolote!* Come here.

(*The Owl enters, flying.*)

The Owl:	(*In a very formal voice.*) Yes, you called, Hormiguita?
Hormiguita:	*Tecolote*, I just saw a mouse run by here. I'm stuck under this snowflake and you can help me by chasing one of your favorite foods. Chase the mouse, until the mouse gnaws at the wall, until the wall blocks the wind, until the wind blows the cloud in the sky, until the cloud covers the sun, until the sun melts the snowflake, until the snowflake gets off my leg, so I can go home.
The Owl:	I beg you pardon? You want me to work when it's not nighttime?
Hormiguita:	It wouldn't be work. It'd be chasing a mouse. That's not work for an owl. That's what owls do!
The Owl:	I will decide what's work and what's not work. And that is work. So I don't think so.
Hormiguita:	Owl, how can you be this way? Oh, you're not worth anything! But someone is going to help me. I just know it. *¡Agua! ¡Agua!* Water! Water!

(*The Cat enters, slowly wandering.*)

The Cat:	Meoooow.
Hormiguita:	*Gato!* Am I glad to see you! See that owl over there? He was making fun of you. Saying that he could bite you whenever he wanted to. I told him that if you were here, you would teach him a lesson. So *gato*, scratch the owl's eyes, until the owl chases the mouse, until the mouse gnaws at the wall, until the wall blocks the wind, until the wind blows the cloud in the sky, until the cloud covers the sun, until the sun melts the snowflake, until the snowflake gets off my leg, so I can go home.
The Cat:	Meooow. (*The cat curls up and goes to sleep.*)
Hormiguita:	*Gato!* Now is no time for a cat nap. Wake up and help me.
The Cat:	Meooow. Too much work. I don't think so.
The Narrator:	Poor Hormiguita. It does look as if no one is going to help her. But there are still a few more parts to her adventure, so don't give up yet, Hormiguita.

(*The Dog enters, sniffing around.*)

Hormiguita:	*Perro!* My old friend *perro*. I remember when you dug up my anthill and we had to build it all over again. All the other ants were mad, but I thought it was funny. It's so good to see you again.

From *¡Teatro! Hispanic Plays for Young People*. Copyright © 1996. Teacher Ideas Press. (800) 237-6124.

(*The Dog sniffs around Hormiguita.*)

Hormiguita:	*Perro*, stop sniffing around and help me. I really need your help. If you help me, I know where some bones are buried. My parents found them when they were digging some new anthill tunnels. See that *gato* sleeping over there? Chase the cat, until the cat scratches the owl's eyes, until the owl chases the mouse, until the mouse gnaws at the wall, until the wall blocks the wind, until the wind blows the cloud in the sky, until the cloud covers the sun, until the sun melts the snowflake, until the snowflake gets off my leg, so I can go home.
The Dog:	Cat's too fast. Already chased it and didn't catch it. Too much work. I don't think so.
Hormiguita:	Oh *perro*! If I had a stick, I'd beat you myself, you big old lazy dog! In fact, I see a stick right here by me now. You're going to get it dog!

(*The Stick enters.*)

Hormiguita:	*Palito*, here's your chance. Beat the dog, until the dog chases the cat, until the cat scratches the owl's eyes, until the owl chases the mouse, until the mouse gnaws at the wall, until the wall blocks the wind, until the wind blows the cloud in the sky, until the cloud covers the sun, until the sun melts the snowflake, until the snowflake gets off my leg, so I can go home.
The Stick:	That dog's too mean. If he gets hold of me, he'll bury me in the ground.
Hormiguita:	He's not that mean
The Stick:	Besides, it's too much work. I don't think so.
The Narrator:	By now, Hormiguita was really giving up hope. She had started to cry when she heard the sound of a little fire crackling nearby. The fire had been left there from a campfire some workers had left in the woods.

(*The Fire enters.*)

Hormiguita:	*Lumbre*, you're my last chance. Please, I ask of you, help me. *Lumbre*, burn the stick, until the stick beats the dog, until the dog chases the cat, until the cat scratches the owl's eyes, until the owl chases the mouse, until the mouse gnaws at the wall, until the wall blocks the wind, until the wind blows the cloud in the sky, until the cloud covers the sun, until the sun melts the snowflake, until the snowflake gets off my leg, so I can go home.
The Fire:	I'm a fire on my way out. There are barely enough embers to burn anything. It's time for me to go out. It would be too much work to get the embers going again. I don't think so.
Hormiguita:	I'm going to die of thirst and no one is going to help me. *¡Agua! ¡Agua! ¡Agua!*

From *¡Teatro! Hispanic Plays for Young People.* Copyright © 1996. Teacher Ideas Press. (800) 237-6124.

| The Narrator: | And then the most amazing thing happened. Out of the earth came a little ground-spring of water, gurgling up to the surface. |

(*The Water enters.*)

| Hormiguita: | *¡Agua!* My prayers have been answered. At last my prayers have been answered. Water, you are just what I need. Water, act like you're going to put out the fire, until the fire burns the stick, until the stick beats the dog, until the dog chases the cat, until the cat scratches the owl's eyes, until the owl chases the mouse, until the mouse gnaws at the wall, until the wall blocks the wind, until the wind blows the cloud in the sky, until the cloud covers the sun, until the sun melts the snowflake, until the snowflake gets off my leg, so I can go home. |
| The Water: | Sure. All that will be fun to see! |

(*As the narrator describes the action, the characters act it out.*)

The Narrator:	And you know what? The water did just what Hormiguita asked. The water pretended to put out the fire, until the fire burned the stick, until the stick beat the dog, until the dog chased the cat, until the cat scratched the owl's eyes, until the owl chased the mouse, until the mouse gnawed at the wall, until the wall blocked the wind, until the wind blew the cloud in the sky, until the cloud covered the sun, until the sun melted the snowflake, until the snowflake got off Hormiguita's leg.
Hormiguita:	I'm free!
The Narrator:	And with those joyful words, Hormiguita ran home.

(*All exit.*)

Scene 3: At the anthill.

(*Father Ant and Mother Ant enter.*)

Father Ant:	Have you seen her at all?
Mother Ant:	Not since the storm came in.
Father Ant:	I told her not to wander off playing.
Mother Ant:	Look, here she comes. She is really running!

(*Hormiguita enters.*)

| Hormiguita: | Mama, papa! I was lost in the forest and a big snowflake fell on me and I was stuck and the sun wouldn't— |

From *¡Teatro! Hispanic Plays for Young People.* Copyright © 1996. Teacher Ideas Press. (800) 237-6124.

Father Ant:	Hormiguita, slow down and catch your breath. I can't understand a word you're saying. Where have you been?
Hormiguita:	That's what I'm trying to tell you. I was yelling for *agua* and . . .

(*All exit, with Hormiguita telling them the story of her adventures*.)

The Narrator:	All that night, Hormiguita told her parents all about her adventures. Her parents asked her if she had learned her lesson, and she told them that she had, especially the one about complaining that work was too hard. From that day on, Hormiguita was one of the hardest workers in the ant colony.

From *¡Teatro! Hispanic Plays for Young People*. Copyright © 1996. Teacher Ideas Press. (800) 237-6124.

The Smelly Feet

Introduction

The Smelly Feet, a delightful and playful animal fable, is another story that offers opportunities for students to invent animal characterizations. Students find these types of stories easy to understand and fun to perform.

Staging

The best preparation for this story is improvisational games that allow students to create animal movements and poses. Another creative activity is to have students invent voices for the different animals.

Props

Wedding presents

Costumes

See figure 6 in the introduction to this book.

Cast of Characters

The Narrator

The Lion

The Bear

Animals of the Forest:

The Dog	The Fox
The Cat	The Spider
The Owl	The Monkey

Scene 1: In the forest.

(As the narrator speaks, The Lion and The Bear enter and pose. They each have a similar walk, which conveys pride and arrogance.)

The Narrator:	Once, in a part of the forest far away from here, there lived a lion. (*The Lion enters, walks around the stage proudly, and strikes a pose.*) Now, as you can see, the lion has what we would call nowadays an attitude. But if you were king of all the animals, you might walk around with an attitude, too. There also lived in the forest a bear. (*The Bear enters, walks around the stage proudly, and strikes a pose.*) Now, as you can see, the bear also has what we would call nowadays an attitude. But if you were as big and as strong as the bear, you might have an attitude, too. Well, it just so happened that one day the bear and the lion met each other, (*The Lion and the Bear turn and look at each other.*) fell in love, (*The Lion and the Bear run and hug each other.*) and got married. (*The Lion and the Bear face front, standing in a marriage pose, holding hands. They exit, holding hands.*) Now you might think this couldn't happen, but I tell you that in this story it did happen. When they heard the good news, all the animals of the forest were so happy for the lion and the bear.

(Animals of the Forest enter, all carrying wedding presents.)

The Dog:	I can't believe that Lion and Bear got married.
The Cat:	Me neither.
The Owl:	Lion has lived alone for so long. It will be hard for him to change his ways and live with someone else.
The Fox:	And Bear is so headstrong. She will never be able to live with someone else.
The Spider:	But I'm happy that they found each other and have a chance for happiness together. Lion was always so lonely. He would walk through the forest all day long by himself looking for food.
The Monkey:	And so was Bear. She would wander through the forest all day long by herself looking for berries to eat.
The Dog:	Well, I hope they stay happy.
The Cat:	So do I.
The Owl:	But how long do you think it will really last?
The Spider:	Will what last?
The Fox:	Their happiness.

From *¡Teatro! Hispanic Plays for Young People.* Copyright © 1996. Teacher Ideas Press. (800) 237-6124.

The Monkey:	I don't know. But I do know that with two headstrong attitudes like theirs, sooner or later there will be . . . well, you know.
The Spider:	No, I don't know. There will be what?
The Monkey:	You know . . . I don't want to say it out loud because it might put a jinx on their happiness.
The Spider:	What kind of jinx?
The Dog:	Spider! Can't you figure it out?
The Spider:	No, I can't. Just tell me.
The Fox:	Okay. Maybe if we all say it out loud together it won't cause a jinx.
The Owl:	I think that's a good idea. Let's try it.
The Cat:	Everybody ready? (*All nod yes.*) Here goes. One. Two. Three.
All Animals of the Forest, except the Spider:	The first argument.
The Spider:	Oh! The first argument!
All Animals of the Forest, except the Spider:	Shhh!

(*All exit.*)

Scene 2: In the home of the lion and the bear.

The Narrator:	One day the lion and the bear had been out looking for food. It had been a very hot day and the lion's feet were burning up from walking around the forest all day. He came home and put his feet up in the air so the cool breeze would cool off those burning feet.

(*The Lion enters, sits down, and puts his feet up in the air.*)

The Lion:	It's too hot. I've been walking through the forest all day long and didn't find any food at all. I hope bear found some food. I'm starving! And my feet are burning up. They're so hot and tired. I'm just going to put them up in the air and let the breeze cool them off.

(*The Bear enters. She stops and sniffs the air. She makes a face as she smells something stinky. She sniffs all around the room, each time coming closer to the Lion. Finally, she is sniffing all around the Lion and discovers the source of the stink.*)

From ¡*Teatro! Hispanic Plays for Young People.* Copyright © 1996. Teacher Ideas Press. (800) 237-6124.

The Bear:	Lion, I have something bad to tell you. Your feet really smell! Go down to the river and wash them off.
The Lion:	My feet do not smell. You must be smelling something else.
The Bear:	I've smelled all over the room and it's your feet that are smelling up the room.

(*Both the Lion and the Bear are trying their hardest to be polite and not start an argument.*)

The Lion:	My feet do not smell. Perhaps, dearest, you made a mistake and you should come back in and start over, dearest!
The Bear:	Perhaps I did make a mistake, dearest. I will go out and come back in and start over, dearest!

(*The Bear exits and returns. She again makes a face as she smells something stinky. She sniffs all around the room and she again ends up sniffing by the Lion.*)

The Bear:	Lion, your feet stink!
The Lion:	My feet do not stink!
The Bear:	They smell terrible. They are stinking up the whole house.
The Lion:	And I'm telling you they do not stink. You are just imagining that they stink.
The Bear:	I am not imagining anything. They stink!
The Lion:	They do not stink!
The Bear:	Stink.
The Lion:	Don't stink.
The Bear:	Stink.
The Lion:	Don't stink.

(*The Lion and the Bear freeze, motionless in their positions.*)

The Narrator:	Well by now you must know what this is. This is what all the animals were talking about—the first argument!

(*The Lion and the Bear start moving again.*)

The Bear:	Stink.
The Lion:	Don't stink.

From *¡Teatro! Hispanic Plays for Young People.* Copyright © 1996. Teacher Ideas Press. (800) 237-6124.

The Bear:	Stink.
The Lion:	Don't stink.
The Bear:	They do stink. And I'll prove it to you. You are king of the beasts. Call all the animals together and we will have them tell us if your feet smell or not.
The Lion:	That's a good idea. I will call all the animals together. And they will tell you they don't stink.
The Bear:	They will tell you they do stink.

(*The Lion and the Bear exit, arguing about what the animals will tell them.*)

Scene 3: Later in the day in the forest.

The Narrator:	So the lion did call all the animals. And if you are an animal in the forest and you hear the lion roaring, you come running. When all the animals had been gathered together, they were excited, because this was the argument they had been expecting. But they did not expect that they would have to be part of the argument.

(*Animals of the Forest enter.*)

The Fox:	Why did Lion call us?
The Dog:	Haven't you heard?
The Spider:	Heard what?
The Cat:	It's what we have been waiting for.
The Spider:	What? Tell me. Tell me.
The Owl:	The first argument.
The Spider:	Oh.
The Monkey:	Shhh! Here they come.

(*The Lion and the Bear enter.*)

The Lion:	I have called you all here today to settle an argument between Bear and myself.
The Owl:	See, I told you.
All Animals of the Forest, except the Owl:	Shhh!

From *¡Teatro! Hispanic Plays for Young People.* Copyright © 1996. Teacher Ideas Press. (800) 237-6124.

The Lion:	I have called you here to come up and smell my feet and tell Bear that they do not stink.
The Bear:	Yes, it is true that he called you here today to smell his feet. But he got one detail wrong. You are to smell his feet and tell him that they do stink.
All Animals of the Forest:	The first argument!
The Lion:	Now, who is going to go first?
The Dog:	I'm the best sniffer in the whole animal kingdom. I'll go first.

(*The Lion puts his feet up in the air and the Dog approaches them and sniffs all around them.*)

The Dog:	Whew! Lion, those feet stink!

(*All Animals of the Forest react with yelps and howls. The Lion cuffs the Dog on the head and the Dog goes rolling to the side. The Dog sits up and rubs his head.*)

The Dog:	Ouch! What happened?
The Lion:	And that is what will happen to whoever says my feet stink! Now who is next?
All Animals of the Forest, except the Dog:	Not me. (*Pointing to another animal.*) Maybe you should go. I don't feel so good. It's your turn.
The Lion:	Cat, you're a really good sniffer. You go next.
The Cat:	(*A little frightened and nervous.*) Sure lion. Whatever you say.

(*The Cat approaches the Lion and sniffs around his feet. She then looks over at the Dog rubbing his head. The Dog shakes his head as if saying "no."*)

The Cat:	You know Lion, I can't smell a thing. They don't stink!

(*As soon as the Cat has spoken, the other Animals of the Forest react with yelps and howls and cheers. The Bear immediately cuffs the Cat on the head and sends the Cat rolling. The Cat sits up and rubs her head.*)

The Cat:	Ouch! What happened?
The Bear:	And that's what will happen to whoever says they don't stink!

From *¡Teatro! Hispanic Plays for Young People.* Copyright © 1996. Teacher Ideas Press. (800) 237-6124.

| The Narrator: | And that is how the rest of the day went. Whenever one of the animals would say the lion's feet did stink, the lion would give the animal a tremendous slap on the head with his mighty paw and say, "They do not stink." And whenever one of the animals would say the lion's feet did not stink, the bear would give the animal a savage blow to the head with her mighty paw and say, "They do stink." Finally, one animal was left—the fox. |

(*All Animals of the Forest, except the Fox, are standing around rubbing their heads.*)

The Dog:	This has been a terrible day.
The Cat:	There is no way to win. No matter what we say, we're going to get hit.
The Owl:	Why did we ever want the first argument to happen?
The Monkey:	I wish they'd never had the first argument.
The Spider:	Me too!
The Lion:	Who's next?
The Bear:	Only one animal left, Lion—Fox.
The Lion:	Then Fox will settle the argument once and for all. Fox, get to smelling.
The Dog:	Fox has something up. I can tell.
The Owl:	Fox is clever. They don't say "sly as a fox" for nothing.
The Cat:	Fox has some good plan. I see it in her eyes.
The Spider:	What is Fox going to do? No matter what you say, you get in trouble.
The Monkey:	Just watch. Old clever Fox will figure a way out.

(*The Fox approaches the Lion and sniffs at his feet but doesn't say anything.*)

| The Lion: | Fox, you better say something! |

(*The Fox sniffs even more this time but still doesn't say anything.*)

| The Bear: | Fox, you better say something! |

(*For a third time, the Fox sniffs even harder but still doesn't say anything.*)

| The Lion and the Bear: | Fox, you better say something, and you better say it now! |

From *¡Teatro! Hispanic Plays for Young People.* Copyright © 1996. Teacher Ideas Press. (800) 237-6124.

The Fox: | I'm sorry Lion, O Mighty King of the Beasts, and Bear, O Most Powerful of the Animals. I have a cold and my nose is all stuffed up. I can't smell a thing. I really can't say if they stink or don't stink!

(*All Animals of the Forest, except the Fox, applaud and react with laughter and howls. The Bear and the Lion stomp off, still arguing.*)

The Narrator: | And to this day, all the animals of the forest tell the story of the day when the fox out-foxed both the lion and the bear.

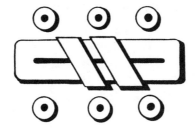

From *¡Teatro! Hispanic Plays for Young People*. Copyright © 1996. Teacher Ideas Press. (800) 237-6124.

The Foolish Coyote

Introduction

This animal fable is a traditional classic appearing in the oral traditions of many cultures. As in all fables, the moral of the story is contained in its closing dramatic events. The clever manipulation of the coyote by the wise old owl presents a clear moral fable on greed and vanity.

In the oral traditions of many cultures, the coyote represents the trickster, the outsider who, through cleverness and boldness, bests authority and breaks cultural rules without punishment. This tale, however, is one of several in the Hispanic tradition that has the coyote as the buffoon and foolish character in the story.

Staging

The best preparation for this story is improvisational games that allow students to create animal movements and poses. Another creative activity is to have students invent voices for the different animals.

Props

None required.

Costumes

See figure 6 in the introduction to this book.

Cast of Characters

The Narrator   Baby Pigeon #3
Coyote   Wise Old Owl
Mama Pigeon   Dove
Baby Pigeon #1   Robin
Baby Pigeon #2

Scene 1: In the forest.

(As the scene begins, Mama Pigeon and the Baby Pigeons are on stage, busy cleaning their feathers.)

| The Narrator: | One day, Coyote was wandering through the fields looking for some food. It had been several days since he had eaten, and he was starving. He was not just a little bit hungry, but he was that kind of hungry when your stomach is rumbling and growling. He tried to chase down several rabbits, but they were too fast. Just as he was about to give up, he spotted a nest in a tree. |

(Coyote enters.)

| Coyote: | I'm so hungry! It's been days since I've had a decent meal. I wish I were a better hunter. Everything I've tried to catch has gotten away. Lion laughed at me. Tiger laughed at me. They think they're the greatest hunters, but one day I'll show them that I'm the greatest hunter. I'm just a little bit down on my luck lately. And hungry. Oh well, I might as well go home. I don't think anything is going to happen today . . . Hey, what's that noise? It's close, very close. *(He searches around the stage.)* It's coming from right over here . . . right over here . . . from right up in that tree. It's a nest full of birds. Nice, fat, baby birds! |

(Mama Pigeon looks out of her nest and sees Coyote.)

Mama Pigeon:	It's Coyote! Baby pigeons, be careful. It's Coyote. He'll eat us all up if he gets the chance.
Coyote:	Just what I was hungry for. Nice, fat, baby pigeons. I must have smelled them with my great hunter's nose. Or seen them with my great hunter's eyes. And now I have them.
Mama Pigeon:	Baby pigeons, stay in the nest. As long as we are up here, he will never be able to get us.
Baby Pigeon #1:	But mama, what if it flies up and gets us?
Mama Pigeon:	Coyotes can't fly.
Baby Pigeon #2:	What if he climbs the tree?
Mama Pigeon:	Coyotes can't climb trees.
Baby Pigeon #3:	What if he chops down the tree?
Mama Pigeon:	Don't even say that. Because then he would get us all and eat us all up.

From *¡Teatro! Hispanic Plays for Young People.* Copyright © 1996. Teacher Ideas Press. (800) 237-6124.

Coyote:	But how will I ever be able to get them down from that tree. Maybe they don't see me and they will come down by themselves. I could hide in the bushes and catch them when they get close. I better check. Mama Pigeon, do you know I'm down here?
Mama Pigeon:	Of course I know you're down there you *loco* coyote. And you're not going to get any of my baby birds!
Coyote:	Oh! She knows I'm down here. (*Thinking deeply.*) There goes that plan . . . ummm, maybe I could . . . no I can't fly . . . maybe I could . . . no I can't climb trees. I know! I could chop down the tree!
Baby Pigeon #1:	Mama, it looks as if Coyote is going to do something.
Baby Pigeon #2:	Look, he is trying to do something.
Baby Pigeon #3:	I'm scared. I'm going to fly away and be safe.
Mama Pigeon:	You can't fly away. You're just learning how to fly. You might not be able to fly high enough to escape. We all have to stay in the nest where we're safe from Coyote.
Coyote:	Mama Pigeon! Throw down one of your baby birds or I'm going to chop down the tree and eat you and all the baby birds.
Baby Pigeon #3:	I told you he was going to chop down the tree.
Mama Pigeon:	He can't chop down the tree. He doesn't even have an ax or anything.
Coyote:	Mama Pigeon! I said throw down one of your baby birds or I'm going to chop down the tree and eat all your babies and you, too!
Baby Pigeon #2:	He means it, mama!
Baby Pigeon #1:	He does!
Mama Pigeon:	Just stay in the nest and we'll be all right.
Coyote:	Okay, now I'm going to chop down the tree with my ax . . . Oh, where is my ax. I left my ax at home! Then I'm going to saw down the tree with my saw . . . Oh, where is my saw! I left my saw at home. What am I going to do? I'm so hungry I can just taste those baby birds. Okay, Mama Pigeon, because you're not throwing down any of those baby birds, I'm going to chop down the tree with my . . . with my . . . (*Frantically looking around for something to chop down the tree with.*) . . . with my . . . tail!
Baby Pigeon #1:	He's going to chop down the tree with his tail!
Baby Pigeon #2:	We'll all be coyote food!
Baby Pigeon #3:	Not me. I'm flying out of here!

From *¡Teatro! Hispanic Plays for Young People.* Copyright © 1996. Teacher Ideas Press. (800) 237-6124.

(Baby Pigeon #3 flies out of the nest. Mama Pigeon tries to stop her but she is determined and gets away. At first she can't fly very well and falls in the direction of Coyote. Coyote thinks that she is a baby pigeon thrown down by Mama Pigeon and tries to catch her. As Coyote almost catches her, she begins to fly better and flies away from Coyote. Coyote chases her but she eventually flies away off stage and Coyote gives up the chase.)

Coyote:	*(Catching his breath.)* Whew! That little bird can really fly. Now I'm too tired to do anything else. I'm so hungry I don't have any energy at all. I need to rest a little while. I'll just rest here for a moment and then I'll get those birds.

(Coyote curls up and falls asleep.)

Scene 2: Later in the day.

(The stage is set as in the beginning of Scene One. The coyote is on one side of the stage. Mama Pigeon and the Baby Pigeons, except for Baby Pigeon # 3, are on the other side of the stage.)

The Narrator:	Coyote was so hungry and tired that he just fell asleep right under Mama Pigeon's tree. Mama Pigeon was so scared and worried that she huddled with her two babies in the nest crying. Soon, however, Wise Old Owl came flying by and, when he saw Mama Pigeon crying, he flew right over to see what was wrong.

(Wise Old Owl enters.)

Wise Old Owl:	Mama Pigeon, what is wrong. I've never seen you crying so hard.
Mama Pigeon:	*(Speaking between sobs.)* Oh, Wise Old Owl, I'm so glad you flew by. Coyote says he is going to chop down the tree and eat us all up. One of my babies has flown away and barely escaped with her life. Now, when Coyote wakes up, he's going to chop down the tree and eat us all up.
Wise Old Owl:	That sounds really terrible. I'm sorry that your baby flew away, but she did escape, don't forget. And Mama Pigeon . . . come over here. Look out of the nest and look at Coyote's tail.
Mama Pigeon:	I can't. It's too scary.
Wise Old Owl:	No it's not. Just look down and tell me about it.
Mama Pigeon:	*(Looking down at Coyote's tail.)* Well it's . . . it's . . . it's kind of furry . . . and mangy looking . . . and soft looking . . . and curled up in a circle . . . Wise Old Owl . . . that tail can't chop down a tree, can it?
Wise Old Owl:	Of course not, Mama Pigeon! There is nothing to be worried about. Next time Coyote says he's going to chop down the tree with his tail, just lean over the edge of the nest and tell him, "Go right ahead."

From *¡Teatro! Hispanic Plays for Young People.* Copyright © 1996. Teacher Ideas Press. (800) 237-6124.

(*Wise Old Owl exits, flying away.*)

Scene 3: Later in the day.

(*The stage is set as in Scenes One and Two.*)

The Narrator:	And with that good advice, Wise Old Owl flew away. As soon as he had gone, Coyote woke up from his nap with just one thing on his mind.
Coyote:	(*Stretching.*) Ahhh, I feel better now. Much better. Now, to get me some baby birds! Mama Pigeon, throw down another baby bird or I'll chop down the tree with my tail and I'll eat you all up.
Mama Pigeon:	(*Leaning over the edge of the nest.*) Go right ahead.
Coyote:	What did you say!
Mama Pigeon:	Go right ahead.
Coyote:	I mean it. I'll chop down this tree with my tail.
Mama Pigeon:	Go right ahead.
Coyote:	Okay, you asked for it. This tree is coming down. (*He winds up his body as if to strike the tree with his tail.*) One . . . I mean it.
Mama Pigeon:	Go right ahead.
Coyote:	Two . . . You better throw down a baby bird!
Mama Pigeon:	Go right ahead.
Coyote:	Three! (*He swings his body hard and hits the tree with his tail.*) OWWWWW! That hurts! (*He exits yelling and holding his tail.*)
Mama Pigeon:	Now, let's go find your sister and tell her that everything is safe and that she can come back to the nest.

(*Mama Pigeon and her babies exit, flying away. Coyote exits, nursing his sore tail.*)

Scene 4: At the river.

(*On one side of the stage sits Coyote, soaking his tail in the river. On the other side of the stage sits Wise Old Owl with two other birds, Dove and Robin. They are all laughing.*)

The Narrator:	Coyote ran down to the river and put his tail into the water. As he was soaking his tail, he heard loud laughter coming from the other side of the river.

From ¡*Teatro! Hispanic Plays for Young People*. Copyright © 1996. Teacher Ideas Press. (800) 237-6124.

Coyote:	Owww. That was the stupidest thing I have ever done. I didn't even get any baby birds. Owwww.

(*Loud laughing is heard.*)

Wise Old Owl:	And there was Coyote sleeping under the tree.
Dove:	And then what happened?
Robin:	I wish I'd been there to see all this. Coyote thinks he's a great hunter but he has to be one of the most foolish animals on earth.
Wise Old Owl:	So then I just told Mama Pigeon to tell that foolish Coyote, "Go right ahead."

(*All laugh.*)

Coyote:	So it was Wise Old Owl who told Mama Pigeon. He's going to be sorry.

(*As the narrator speaks, the characters act out the scene.*)

The Narrator:	Coyote was angry that it was Wise Old Owl who had told Mama Pigeon what to do. He very quietly began to sneak up on the birds. Creeping ever so softly, he got as close as he could to the birds and just waited for the chance to pounce.
Dove:	And then what did Coyote do?
Wise Old Owl:	He tried to chop down the tree with his tail!
Robin:	That Coyote is crazy. Didn't he know that would hurt?
Dove:	I guess not!

(*All laugh even harder. As they are laughing, Coyote leaps at them and catches Wise Old Owl. Dove and Robin fly away.*)

Coyote:	I caught you!
Wise Old Owl:	Coyote, what are you going to do?
Coyote:	I'm going to eat you to take the place of those baby birds I didn't get to eat because of you.
Wise Old Owl:	Coyote, I can't believe you caught me. No coyote's ever caught me before.
Coyote:	But I did!
Wise Old Owl:	Coyote, your teeth are so sharp . . . Let's not rush things here.
Coyote:	Everyone makes fun of me and says I'm not a good hunter, but if they could only see that I caught Wise Old Owl.

From *¡Teatro! Hispanic Plays for Young People*. Copyright © 1996. Teacher Ideas Press. (800) 237-6124.

Wise Old Owl:	Oh that gives me a good idea, Coyote.
Coyote:	What type of idea?
Wise Old Owl:	An idea about how everybody could know what a great hunter you are. They have to see that you have caught me before you eat me.
Coyote:	That's a good idea! If I eat you first, then nobody will ever believe that I really did catch you.
Wise Old Owl:	Just what I was thinking. But if they see me first, then you will be known far and wide as the best hunter.
Coyote:	Even better than Lion and Tiger.
Wise Old Owl:	Even better.
Coyote:	But how will they see that I've caught you.
Wise Old Owl:	That's the best part of my plan. See that high hill over there?
Coyote:	Yup.
Wise Old Owl:	Take me over to the highest part of the hill. Call all the animals over. As soon as they see that you have caught me, they will call you the greatest hunter and then you can eat me.
Coyote:	That's a good idea!
Wise Old Owl:	I really hope it is. Now take me over to the hill.
Coyote:	Now, don't try anything like trying to escape or I'll eat you right on the spot.
Wise Old Owl:	I wouldn't think of trying to escape from such a mighty hunter as you, Coyote.

(*As the narrator speaks, the characters act out the scene.*)

The Narrator:	As soon as Coyote and Wise Old Owl had reached the top of the hill, Wise Old Owl told Coyote—
Wise Old Owl:	Now call out so everyone can see what a great hunter you are!
The Narrator:	And as soon as Coyote opened his mouth, Wise Old Owl flew away. Wise Old Owl than flew around Coyote's head, taunting him.
Wise Old Owl:	Coyote, you're a fool!
The Narrator:	And you know what? Coyote was a fool!

From *¡Teatro! Hispanic Plays for Young People.* Copyright © 1996. Teacher Ideas Press. (800) 237-6124.

Part III
Holiday Plays

El Día de Los Muertos
The Fiesta of the Day of the Dead

Introduction

El Día de Los Muertos, The Fiesta of the Day of the Dead, is a celebration during which families remember and honor relatives who have died. The celebration of the Day of the Dead is a blending of religious practices of two major cultures—the Mexican Aztec and the Spanish Catholic.

The Aztecs believed that death and life were closely intertwined. They had a complex cosmology that reflected their beliefs about the afterlife. Part of their beliefs included the idea that on certain days of the year, the dead returned to earth to visit the living. The dead returned to earth to see that family and friends were okay and to see that they were remembered. On these days, families would hold celebrations to pay their respects to the dead. These celebrations included the preparation of favorite foods to make an offering to the visiting family members.

When the Spanish came to the New World, they brought with them the customs of All Saint's Day and All Soul's Day. These European and Catholic customs were religious days dedicated to praying for the souls of departed family members and friends. November 1 was All Hallows or All Saints Day. November 2 was All Souls Day. October 31 was All Hallows Eve, which eventually became secularized into Halloween.

It was one of the coincidences of history that the customs from two such different cultures overlapped on the calendar. In time, the ancient Aztec and the Spanish Catholic customs merged in the New World into the Mexican celebration we know as the Day of the Dead.

Today, the Day of the Dead, celebrated November 1 and 2, is both a public and private celebration. In Mexican rural communities, it is a family-centered fiesta marked with food, celebration, and vigils at the cemetery. In American urban settings families, communities, and artists have given the fiesta renewed meaning with processionals, community celebrations, and art gallery shows.

A special mention must be made that even though the Day of the Dead is right next to Halloween, the two holidays evolved from two very different cultural traditions. The two have very different meanings and practices, and should not be confused as similar celebrations, especially in the experiences of children. Now a secular holiday, Halloween centers on the primary activities of costumes, parties, and children's trick-or-treating and is detached from its original connection to religious observances. The Day of the Dead is a powerful, almost ritual, celebration in which families take time to pause to honor and celebrate the memory of those who have passed away.

There are many books describing in more detail the origins and practices of the Day of the Dead celebration and its meaning in Mexican and Mexican-American communities. The bibliography lists several good reference sources for further information.

Staging

This play centers on the preparations of a family for its celebration of *El Día de Los Muertos*. It is meant to be educational and informative in that by performing and experiencing the play, students will learn the primary practices and customs of the Day of the Dead celebrations. The play's central activity is the building of the *ofrenda*, the offering and memorial altar. Though there are other activities associated with *El Día de Los Muertos*, the creation of an *ofrenda* is of primary significance in both Mexican and Mexican-American practices. As a unifying dramatic event, the play's activity involves the construction of what technically becomes a set piece, but will actually become the *ofrenda*. Figure 10 represents a typical *ofrenda*.

Fig. 10. The Day of the Dead *Ofrenda*.

The production of this particular play with students is rich with the possibility of numerous craft activities to make the props of the play. Also, students who are not in the performance of the play could participate in the play's experience by making the props that are called for in the script. An excellent resource book for these activities and the building of the *ofrenda* is *Indo-Hispanic Folk Art Traditions, vol. II* by Bobbi Salinas-Norman.

The play is set in modern times. The set is the interior of a house, which can be indicated by chairs and tables.

Props

Newspaper comics	Scissors
Table	Loaves of *pan de muerto* bread
Long cornstalks	Skeleton masks
Marigold flowers	Small votive candles
Sheets of colored paper	Matches

Costumes

Modern-day costumes. Cast members can wear character-appropriate clothing from home or from a secondhand store.

Cast of Characters

The Sanchez Family:

Jimmy, *a young boy*	Papa, *Jimmy's father*
Gabriella, *Jimmy's older sister*	Tia Juanita, *Jimmy's aunt*
Mama, *Jimmy's mother*	Tio Joe, *Jimmy's uncle*

Scene 1: At the home of the Sanchez family in a modern city.

(At the start of the scene, Gabriella and Jimmy are sitting, eating breakfast and reading the newspaper comics.)

Jimmy:	Hey, I'm reading the comics!
Gabriella:	No you weren't. (*Gabriella takes the comics away from Jimmy.*) I had them first.
Jimmy:	Mama! Gabriella took the comics away from me.
Gabriella:	(*Shoving the comics at her brother.*) Here! I read them already anyway.
Jimmy:	You can have them when I'm done.
Gabriella:	I said I've already read them. Besides, I have to help Mama get ready for *El Día de Los Muertos*. We're going shopping for a few things we need.
Jimmy:	Oh man, I forgot! Papa wanted me to go with him to get the wood for the *ofrenda*.
Gabriella:	Smooth move. I'll just tell him you were too busy reading the comics.
Jimmy:	How could I forget? I told him I wanted to help build the *ofrenda* this year.
Gabriella:	Well, you are finally old enough to be of some real help. In the past, all we did was try to keep you out of the way.
Jimmy:	No way! Last year Mama let me mix the dough for the *pan de muerto* and I got to light the *copal*. I did lots of things.
Gabriella:	Sure you did. But this year I guess your contribution will be reading the comics. (*She laughs.*)
Jimmy:	Mama! Gabriella is making fun of me.
Gabriella:	Fine. Just try to get me in trouble all the time. You don't even know what *El Día de Los Muertos* is really about. You still get it confused with Halloween.
Jimmy:	I don't either.
Gabriella:	Yes you do.
Jimmy:	No I don't.
Gabriella:	Then tell me what it is about.
Jimmy:	It's about . . . it's about . . .
Gabriella:	See, I knew you didn't even know.

From ¡*Teatro! Hispanic Plays for Young People*. Copyright © 1996. Teacher Ideas Press. (800) 237-6124.

Jimmy:	It's about building the *ofrenda* and decorating it.
Gabriella:	But why do we build it?
Jimmy:	Because Mama and Papa want to. That's why.
Gabriella:	Well, you better find out soon. Because this year you're old enough to add something to the *ofrenda* yourself. I already know what I'm going to do.
Jimmy:	What are you going to do?
Gabriella:	I'm not telling.
Jimmy:	I won't tell.
Gabriella:	I'm not worried about you telling. I'm worried about you copying!
Jimmy:	I won't copy.
Gabriella:	All I'm saying is that it's very important to think about what you are going to add to the *ofrenda*. We're making one for our *abuelos* this year and you can't just put anything up there.
Jimmy:	I miss *abuelita*. I wish she hadn't died.
Gabriella:	I miss her, too. I remember when she used to help us with the *ofrenda*, and now we're making one for her. She used to make one for her mother.
Jimmy:	And that's why we're making one for her?
Gabriella:	That's part of it.
Jimmy:	Gabriella, are *ofrendas* only for dead people?
Gabriella:	Of course. They help us remember out relatives who have passed away.
Jimmy:	Do they really come back and visit us?
Gabriella:	That's what people say. (*She leans forward and makes a ghost noise and waves her hand in front of his face.*) Wooooooo.
Jimmy:	Gabriella, that's Halloween stuff. I really do know the difference, you know.
Gabriella:	Hey, lighten up. It was just a joke.
Jimmy:	But how can they come back and visit us? They're dead.
Gabriella:	That's just part of it. Look, according to old stories during this time of year, the dead come back to visit the living.
Jimmy:	Why would they want to do that?
Gabriella:	To see if you've been good to your sister! (*She laughs.*)

From *¡Teatro! Hispanic Plays for Young People.* Copyright © 1996. Teacher Ideas Press. (800) 237-6124.

Jimmy:	No, really!
Gabriella:	I mean it. They come back to see how we are doing and to see if we remember them.
Jimmy:	I'll never forget *abuelita*.
Gabriella:	Then you better start thinking about what you're going to add to the *ofrenda*. Because that's the way you'll show how you remember her. Oh, and by the way, I don't think putting the comics on the *ofrenda* is a good idea! (*She laughs and exits, darting away as Jimmy tries to hit her with the comics. He exits, chasing her.*)

Scene 2: The setting is a room in the house. There are a few pieces of furniture with an open space large enough for the construction of the altar.

(*Tio Joe enters with Papa. They are carrying a table and some long cornstalks.*)

Tio Joe:	So what happened to Jimmy? I thought he was going to help us this year.
Papa:	I don't know. He was going to join us after breakfast, but I guess he got busy and forgot.
Tio Joe:	Well let's get the *ofrenda* started. Let's put the table here.

(*They put the table in the middle of the stage.*)

Papa:	That's good. Now, give me the cornstalks.

(*Jimmy enters, running. During the dialogue that follows, Tio Joe and Papa, with the help of Jimmy, braid the cornstalks and make an arch in front of the table.*)

Jimmy:	Papa, I'm sorry. I was eating breakfast and then Gabriella and I got in a fight and then—
Papa:	That's all right, *jito*. But if you tell someone that you're going to help, then it's your responsibility to be there.
Tio Joe:	Especially this year. This year you are going to be a big help with the *ofrenda*.
Jimmy:	I want to be a big help.
Papa:	Well then, help hold these cornstalks while we braid them.
Jimmy:	Papa, Gabriella said that this year we are making the *ofrenda* for *abuelita*.

From *¡Teatro! Hispanic Plays for Young People*. Copyright © 1996. Teacher Ideas Press. (800) 237-6124.

Papa:	She's one of the people we're making it for this year. This is the first celebration of *El Día de Los Muertos* since she passed away.
Jimmy:	Tio, who are you celebrating this year?
Tio Joe:	Oh, I have a lot of people to celebrate. When you're as old as I am, there are a lot of people to remember this time of year. My *padre* and *madre*. My favorite brother, Alonso.
Jimmy:	When you were a little boy, did you do *ofrendas*?
Tio Joe:	Oh yes. Every year. Your Tia Juanita always made sure that we made one. I remember one year, we stayed up all night the night before making *tamales*, *pan de muerto*, *tortillas*. I can smell all that good food right now! Here, help me hold up these cornstalks to see if they are tall enough. (*They hold up two braided cornstalks.*) There, they are almost enough. Just a couple more and we'll be able to make the arch.

(*Gabriella, Mama, and Tia Juanita enter. They are carrying marigold flowers.*)

Papa:	Oh good, you were able to get the flowers.
Mama:	They were almost sold out.
Tia Juanita:	In Mexico, we never had to go to the store to buy the marigolds. They just grew and we just picked them. Bright yellow and orange flowers growing everywhere . . . Oh the arch is looking good. Jimmy, how are things going here?
Jimmy:	Fine, Tia. We are almost through with the arch.
Tio Joe:	(*Putting up the arch against the table.*) We are through. There, how does it look?
Mama:	I don't think it's tall enough.
Papa:	That's as tall as it's going to be. We're not in Mexico where I could just go out and cut some more.
Mama:	When I was a little girl, we would use long sugarcane for the arch. But these will do, I guess. Gabriella, come and help me in the kitchen. We have to finish the cooking.
Gabriella:	Okay, Mama.
Tio Joe:	I'll come and help be the tester. Nothing like fresh *tortillas* right off the grill.

(*Mama, Gabriella, and Tio Joe exit.*)

From *¡Teatro! Hispanic Plays for Young People*. Copyright © 1996. Teacher Ideas Press. (800) 237-6124.

| Papa: | Maybe it is too short. I'm going to go see if I can find more cornstalks. *Jito*, you stay and keep your *tia* company. (*He exits.*) |

(*Tia Juanita and Jimmy sit. During the dialogue that follows, they make paper cut-outs.*)

Tia Juanita:	(*Giving Jimmy some sheets of colorful paper and scissors.*) Here Jimmy, here are some sheets of paper. You can help me make the *papel picado*.
Jimmy:	Oh boy, this is fun. I always like the *papel picado*.
Tia Juanita:	Well, do a careful job. They will help decorate the *ofrenda*.
Jimmy:	Tia, Gabriella was telling me that the dead are coming to visit us.
Tia Juanita:	Well, that's true Jimmy.

(*There is a silence while Jimmy thinks.*)

Jimmy:	I'm a little scared, Tia.
Tia Juanita:	Scared! About what?
Jimmy:	Well . . . you know . . .
Tia Juanita:	No, I don't know. Why don't you tell me?
Jimmy:	About the dead people coming. (*Getting excited.*) I saw in this movie once. The Lost Island. These people went and found a lost city, and when they tried to take the gold away, the dead people of the lost city came after them and they were all—
Tia Juanita:	Jimmy! *El Día de Los Muertos* is not a movie. Especially not one like that. What an imagination you have.
Jimmy:	But it scared me, Tia.
Tia Juanita:	But *El Día de Los Muertos* is not like that.
Jimmy:	Gabriella's right. I'm just stupid, and I'll never know about it all.
Tia Juanita:	You're not stupid. This is just the first year you're old enough to really be part of the family celebration. You'll learn as we go along.
Jimmy:	Is that how you learned?
Tia Juanita:	Of course. Now let's see how you are doing. (*She inspects the cut-outs he has made so far.*) You're doing a very good job. See, you're learning already. Everything we do is all part of a long line of traditions. I did them before you. My mother did them before me. And her mother did them before her. And your children will do them after we are long gone.

From *¡Teatro! Hispanic Plays for Young People.* Copyright © 1996. Teacher Ideas Press. (800) 237-6124.

Jimmy:	Then, they'll make *ofrendas* for us, won't they?
Tia Juanita:	Of course they will. The ancient Aztecs in Mexico believed that it was important to remember our passed-away relatives. They are the ones who gave us the tradition of remembering like this. And in church, we learned that All Saint's Day and All Soul's Day are the days we pray for the dead that their souls may be resting in peace.
Jimmy:	And by making the *ofrenda*, it helps us remember doesn't it?
Tia Juanita:	Yes it does. And it always makes me happy to remember how much I loved them. And how much they loved me.
Jimmy:	I'll always remember you, Tia. (*Holding up a cut-out.*) Look at this one. It's perfect!

(*Gabriella enters with a large basket of* pan de muerto.)

Gabriella:	Jimmy, that's really nice. Here is the *pan de muerto.* We could barely keep Tio Joe's hand off of them as they came out of the oven.
Jimmy:	I can barely keep my hands off of them, they smell so good.
Gabriella:	Well you better. That would be just like you. Eat all the *pan de muerto* before the company comes.
Jimmy:	Who is coming!
Tia Juanita:	Your other *tias* and *tios.* They want to remember your *abuelita*, too.
Gabriella:	Jimmy, did you bring home those masks you made in school?
Jimmy:	I almost forgot! They're in my room.
Tia Juanita:	What kind of masks?
Jimmy:	We made *El Día de Los Muertos* masks in schools. And *calaveras* from papier-mâché. I'll go get them. (*He exits.*)

(*Tia Juanita and Gabriella begin to hang the cut-outs on the table.*)

Gabriella:	Has he been bugging you with questions?
Tia Juanita:	Not too many.
Gabriella:	He is so curious this year. Why this? Why that?
Tia Juanita:	You need to be more patient, Gabriella. You were the same way when you were his age.
Gabriella:	No way. I was never like him.

From *¡Teatro! Hispanic Plays for Young People.* Copyright © 1996. Teacher Ideas Press. (800) 237-6124.

Tia Juanita:	Just like him. (*Making fun of her in a kind way, she mimics Gabriella's voice for each question and answers in an exasperated voice*.) What do the marigolds do? The marigolds are the flowers of the dead. They mark the path so our relatives can find the *ofrenda*, Gabriella. Why the food? So there is nourishment for them after their long journey, Gabriella. Why the candles? So there is light in the darkness to light the way for the returning spirits, Gabriella. Why are the church bells ringing? To celebrate that the spirits of the dead are on their way home, Gabriella. Who will eat all the food? We will, and the guests who come to help us celebrate, Gabriella. What can go on the *ofrenda*? Food, something personal, holy cards, fruit, flowers. Almost anything if it is important to you, Gabriella. Why, why, why. If fact, I think you were even worse than your brother.
Gabriella:	Was I afraid of the dead people coming back? (*She makes the ghost sound again and waves her hands*.) Wooooo.
Tia Juanita:	Gabriella, don't make fun of your brother like that.

(*Jimmy enters, carrying a handful of papier-mâché skeleton masks*.)

Jimmy:	Here are the masks, Tia.
Tia Juanita:	Why, they are wonderful! Now everything is starting to be ready. Jimmy, let's put up the *papel picado* and the masks. Gabriella, you put some marigolds in the cornstalks and spread some on the altar. And put some in front of the altar, too. Oh, and don't forget to arrange the *pan de muerto* on the table in a nice way.

(*They finish decorating the table. Then they all stand back to admire it*.)

Tia Juanita:	There, that is looking really nice. Your *abuelita* will really enjoy it.

(*All exit*.)

Scene 3: The room in which the ofrenda is being built.

(*Papa and Mama enter*.)

Mama:	Look! They've done such a wonderful job on the *ofrenda* this year. *Abuelita* will really like it.
Papa:	We have to get ready to go to the procession. I'm carrying the *incensario* this year. Are the kids ready?
Mama:	Gabriella! Jimmy!
Gabriella:	(*From off-stage*.) Just a minute!
Papa:	Well hurry up. And where is your brother?

From *¡Teatro! Hispanic Plays for Young People*. Copyright © 1996. Teacher Ideas Press. (800) 237-6124.

Gabriella:	(*From off-stage.*) Jimmy! It's time to go on the procession.
Mama:	This is almost the part I like the best. I love making the *ofrenda*, but I really enjoy the procession. The whole community walking together, singing, and praying. Saying prayers to *los ancianos,* the old people.
Papa:	(*Laughing to himself.*) The smoke from the *incensario* burning your eyes!
Mama:	That's why I won't carry it. I love the smell of the *copal*, but the smoke burns my eyes if I'm carrying it.
Papa:	Gabriella! Jimmy! Let's go.

(*Gabriella enters, bounding into the room.*)

Papa:	Where's your brother?
Gabriella:	He's in his room sulking.
Mama:	What about? I thought he'd had a good day helping with the *ofrenda*.
Gabriella:	Oh, I made the mistake of telling him he better have something for the *ofrenda*. And because he doesn't have anything now he's all upset and he thinks that *abuelita* won't like the *ofrenda* because of him.
Papa:	Jimmy! We're leaving for the processional. You get out here right now.

(*Jimmy enters, sulking.*)

Mama:	Jimmy, what's wrong?
Jimmy:	Everyone had something for the *ofrenda* but me. I'm going to ruin the *ofrenda*.
Papa:	That's not true.
Jimmy:	Yes it is true. Tia put some special embroidered napkins she made for *abuelita* on the *ofrenda*. Tio put a *Calavera Catrina* mask he got in Mexico on it. Gabriella put some of *abuelita*'s pictures on it. Mama made the *pan de muerto* and *tamales*. You made the altar.
Gabriella:	But you helped with the *papel picado* and the—
Jimmy:	But I don't have anything from me for *abuelita*. She'll think I don't remember her.
Papa:	She'll know you remember her. But for now we have to get to the procession. I'm carrying the *incensario* with the *copal*, and what's a procession without an *incensario*! You'll get over it. Now let's go.

(*All exit.*)

From *¡Teatro! Hispanic Plays for Young People*. Copyright © 1996. Teacher Ideas Press. (800) 237-6124.

Scene 4: *The room with the* ofrenda.

(Tia Juanita and Tio Joe enter.)

Tia Juanita:	Where is everybody? The church bells have started ringing. We have to light the candles on the *ofrenda*. Here, help me.

(They put little votive candles on the ofrenda *and light them.)*

Tio Joe:	I think everybody went on the procession.
Tia Juanita:	They'll be back soon. Once the bells start ringing, it is the beginning of *El Día de Los Muertos* celebrations.

(Papa, Mama, Jimmy, and Gabriella enter.)

Tio Joe:	So how was it?
Mama:	I really enjoyed it. There were more people than ever. We walked by the church and said some special prayers to *los ancianos*. This year, everybody sang and prayed to *los angelitos* we have lost this year.
Gabriella:	The Aztec *conchero* dancers even showed up.
Papa:	It was wonderful. Some kids even carried an arch covered with marigold flowers at the front of the procession.
Mama:	But you put too much *copal* in the *incensario*. You nearly smoked everybody out.
Papa:	We already were outside. Nobody even noticed it at all.
Mama:	That's not what I heard.
Gabriella:	I think you did a great job, Papa.
Papa:	Thanks *jita*.
Tia Juanita:	Well, now it's time for the *fiesta*. We cooked all day just for this moment. And pretty soon, the spirits of our loved ones will be here. Let's just stand and look at our beautiful *ofrenda* before we go eat.

(All circle the ofrenda.)

Jimmy:	Papa, are they here yet?
Papa:	Who?
Jimmy:	The dead people.
Gabriella:	Oh brother!

From *¡Teatro! Hispanic Plays for Young People*. Copyright © 1996. Teacher Ideas Press. (800) 237-6124.

Mama:	Gabriella! Shhh! Jimmy, what do you mean?
Jimmy:	I want to know if *abuelita* is here yet. I have something for her.
Tio Joe:	Just put it on the *ofrenda*, Jimmy. That's why we made it. She'll know it's there for her.

(*Jimmy reaches into his pocket and takes out a letter. He unfolds it and reads it. Then he puts it on the* ofrenda.)

Mama:	What was that, Jimmy?
Jimmy:	It's a letter *abuelita* wrote me once. I've always kept it, and whenever I'm sad and I miss her, I get it out and read it. It's my most precious memory of her.
Gabriella:	That's really . . . you know . . . something special, Jimmy. You're lucky you have such a special thing to put on the *ofrenda*.
Jimmy:	You know what? Right now, it feels as if *abuelita* is here with us right now.
Papa:	The *ofrenda* and all the love for *abuelita* we put into it makes you feel that way.
Mama:	See, *abuelita* has returned to us for just a little while.
Jimmy:	I'm not afraid of *El Día de Los Muertos* anymore. Now I now what all of you were trying to tell me.
Tio Joe:	And now, *la fiesta.* *¡Vamos a comer!*

(*All exit.*)

From *¡Teatro! Hispanic Plays for Young People.* Copyright © 1996. Teacher Ideas Press. (800) 237-6124.

La Aparicion de Nuestra Señora de Guadalupe
The Miracle of Our Lady of Guadalupe

Introduction

La Aparicíon de Nuestra Señora de Guadalupe, The Miracle of Our Lady of Guadalupe, was one of many plays known to Spanish colonialists of the Hispanic Southwest. The play was a dramatic account of the historical and legendary appearance of the Virgin Mary to an Aztec man, Juan Diego, on a hill in Mexico, December 9–12, 1531.

After the conquest of the Aztecs by Cortez in 1521, Spanish missionaries were active in their mission to convert Aztec society to a Hispanic and Catholic society. The legend of the Virgin of Guadalupe is an example of how the Spanish missionaries combined Catholic beliefs with indigenous culture sites and ceremonies to facilitate the Aztec's conversion to Catholicism.

The story of the Virgin of Guadalupe takes place on a hill named Tepeyác. The hill of Tepeyác was the site of an Aztec shrine to the Aztec Mother Goddess Tonantzín, the protector of earth and corn. Before the conquest by Cortez, the Aztecs had come to the shrine of Tonantzín to pray and seek cures. After the Spanish built a shrine to the Virgin on the same spot, the Aztecs continued to come to the site as they had before the conquest. The Spanish eased the Aztec's religious transition to the Virgin by creating paintings in which the Virgin looked like an Aztec princess and by saying that she spoke in Nahuatl, the Aztec language.

Through the following centuries, the story of the miracle of the Virgin of Guadalupe became widely dispersed and believed among all levels of Hispanic culture. The Pope recognized the Virgin of Guadalupe in 1754 as patroness of New Spain. In 1910, she became the patroness of Latin America and, in 1959, she became the Mother of the Americas. Today, the image of the Virgin, surrounded by a wreath of roses and enveloped by the sun's rays, is a powerful artistic, religious, and cultural icon in Hispanic culture. For many Hispanics, December 12, the Feast Day of Our Lady of Guadalupe, marks the beginning of the Christmas season.

Staging

The play takes place in two settings. One interior and one exterior. The interior room is the inside of the Bishop's church. A few pieces of furniture are sufficient to suggest this place. The exterior scenes are on a hill. An open space best suggests this location.

Props

A *tilma,* a kind of poncho (the *tilma* has the image of the Virgin of Guadalupe inside it).
Roses

Costumes

See figures 1, 2, and 8 in the introduction to this book.

Cast of Characters

The Narrator	Brother Thomas
Juan Diego	Sister Carmen
The Holy Mother	The Bishop

Scene 1: On the hill of Tepeyác near the Aztec shrine to Tonantzín.

The Narrator:	The year is 1531. It has been ten years since the mighty battles between Cortez and his soldiers and the Aztec warriors have ended. The soldiers and warriors have put down their weapons. A poor Aztec man, Juan Diego, has recently converted to Christianity. It was his usual practice to go to the church for religious instruction. His church was not in his village but in Tlatelolco, a village just outside Mexico City. His usual path took him by the houses in the village, but this morning, for some reason, he decided to walk over the hill of Tepeyác

(*Juan Diego enters, walking but tired.*)

Juan Diego:	I must rest here for just a moment. I have been hurrying so much, and I am tired from the journey. I'm unfamiliar with this path because I usually take the longer, more traveled road to the village. And the journey on this cold winter day is not as easy as it is in the warmer seasons. This hill is Tepeyác. Nearby is the shrine to Tonantzín, the goddess of the earth and corn. Maybe I should stop and ask Tonantzín to help my sick uncle. No, that wouldn't be right. The days of Tonantzín are over. It's been ten years since the man Cortez came with his soldiers. So much has changed since then. The *padres* have taught me to be a Christian now, so I should continue on to see the *padre*. (*He looks around as if hearing a strange sound.*) What is that sound . . . It seems to be coming from around here somewhere. But I'm the only one here. Maybe someone has also stopped to rest for a moment. (*He looks around but finds no one.*) That sound. It sounds like singing. Like the singing we do in church, singing the holy praises to the Lord. But even more beautiful, and the voices seem to be moving around me like the wind itself.
The Holy Mother:	(*The Virgin of Guadalupe calls from off-stage, calling as if from a distance.*) Juan. Juan.
Juan Diego:	Who is calling my name?
The Holy Mother:	Juan. Juan.
Juan Diego:	It must be the voices of the heavenly angels, or else I have been out in the cold for too long and I am imagining voices.

(*The Holy Mother enters.*)

The Holy Mother:	Juan. Juan
Juan Diego:	(*Seeing the Holy Mother.*) It's a miracle! Her clothes are shining like the sun, and she is surrounded by heavenly light. The singing voices are the voices of the angels themselves! (*He falls to his knees to pray.*)

From ¡*Teatro! Hispanic Plays for Young People.* Copyright © 1996. Teacher Ideas Press. (800) 237-6124.

The Holy Mother:	Juan, I have chosen you to deliver a message to the Bishop at the cathedral.
Juan Diego:	But beautiful Holy Mother, I am a poor farmer. I am not worthy to deliver a message to the Bishop. Why have you chosen me?
The Holy Mother:	I am the Blessed Virgin Mary, the mother of the Lord Jesus Christ. Just know that I have chosen you to be my messenger in this earth.
Juan Diego:	But what am I to do?
The Holy Mother:	Go to the Bishop and tell him that he is to build a church for me here on top of this hill.
Juan Diego:	The Bishop will never listen to a poor farmer.
The Holy Mother:	The church is to be a shrine that will show my love for all my people. Go give my message to the Bishop.
Juan Diego:	The Bishop will never see me. I have only seen the Bishop myself once in a procession during Holy Week.
The Holy Mother:	Juan, I have chosen you to be my messenger. Go and give my message to the Bishop. (*She exits.*)
Juan Diego:	Yes, I will, Holy Mother. (*After the Virgin has left.*) Why has she chosen me to go see the Bishop? (*He exits.*)

Scene 2: At the cathedral.

The Narrator:	Juan Diego hurried to the cathedral. He did not know what he would tell the Bishop or if he would even get to see the Bishop. But he knew he had been given a holy mission from heaven itself.

(*Juan Diego enters.*)

Juan Diego:	(*Looking up at the immense size of the cathedral.*) How did this ever happen to me? And why? I was on my way to the church to pray for my sick uncle, and now I'm in front of the cathedral waiting to see the Bishop. Maybe I was just imagining the Holy Mother. Maybe the cold was playing tricks on my mind.

(*Brother Thomas and Sister Carmen enter.*)

Brother Thomas:	You have asked to see the Bishop?
Juan Diego:	Yes. Please excuse me, but I am on a holy mission and I must see the Bishop.
Sister Carmen:	A holy mission. We don't get to see many people on holy missions. Who are you to be on a holy mission?

From *¡Teatro! Hispanic Plays for Young People.* Copyright © 1996. Teacher Ideas Press. (800) 237-6124.

Juan Diego:	My name is Juan Diego. I am a poor Aztec farmer.
Brother Thomas:	What kind of holy mission?
Juan Diego:	I have witnessed a miracle.
Brother Thomas:	Even better. A miracle!
Sister Carmen:	What kind of miracle?
Juan Diego:	My message is for the Bishop. I really shouldn't tell anyone else.
Brother Thomas:	But we won't know if you should be allowed to see the Bishop if we don't know what the miracle was.
Sister Carmen:	The Bishop is a very busy person, and he doesn't have time to see everyone who walks up to the cathedral asking to see him.
Brother Thomas:	Have you talked to your village *padre* about this miracle? They are usually the ones to talk to the Bishop.
Juan Diego:	I was on the way to the church in Tlatelolco to pray for my sick uncle when I stopped to rest on the hill of Tepeyác. That's when the miracle happened.
Sister Carmen:	Well then, what type of miracle?
Juan Diego:	Can I see the Bishop? I am on a holy mission and I need to deliver the message to him only. The Holy Mother herself gave me the message.
Brother Thomas:	(*Holding back laughter.*) The Holy Mother herself! That is indeed quite a miracle. I wonder why the Holy Mother would ask a poor Aztec farmer to deliver the message when she could just talk to the Bishop herself.
Juan Diego:	But I'm telling the truth. I did see her!
Sister Carmen:	And what was the message the Holy Mother gave you that was so important that she came all the way down from heaven?
Juan Diego:	Now you are starting to make fun of me. But I know I am on a holy mission and that I must see the Bishop.
Sister Carmen:	Wait here. I will see what the Bishop says. (*She exits.*)
Brother Thomas:	Have you ever seen the Bishop?
Juan Diego:	Only in a procession during Holy Week.
Brother Thomas:	Well, if you get to see him, you must look better. Dust off you clothes. (*Juan Diego dusts off his clothes.*) And remember to show you respect. The Bishop is closer to God than all of us.

(*Sister Carmen enters.*)

From *¡Teatro! Hispanic Plays for Young People.* Copyright © 1996. Teacher Ideas Press. (800) 237-6124.

Sister Carmen:	The Bishop says he will see you.

(Sister Carmen and Brother Thomas shrug their shoulders in disbelief as the Bishop enters.)

Juan Diego:	Your Holy Excellency, thank you for seeing me. I am Juan Diego and I have a message for you.
The Bishop:	Tell me about this miracle you have seen.
Juan Diego:	I was walking on the hill of Tepeyác when I heard the most beautiful singing I have ever heard. It was like the heavenly angels were singing. Then she appeared to me. The Holy Mother. She was surrounded by heavenly light and she was the most beautiful vision I have ever seen.
The Bishop:	What did she say to you?
Juan Diego:	She asked me to deliver a message to you. She wants you to build a shrine to her on Tepeyác. The shrine will be a sign to all of us of her love for us.
The Bishop:	Your story is incredible. Imagine the Holy Mother appearing on a hill with a message for me to build a church! Go, for now and I will think about it. *(He exits.)*
Brother Thomas:	You can go now. And don't bother the Bishop with any more of your stories.

(Brother Thomas and Sister Carmen exit.)

Juan Diego:	I have failed in my holy mission. The Bishop didn't believe me. I have let the Holy Mother down. *(He exits.)*

Scene 3: The hill of Tepeyác.

The Narrator:	Juan Diego returned to Tepeyác. He was dejected because he felt he had failed in his mission. He knew that the Bishop's helpers had laughed at him, and that the Bishop did not believe him. When he returned to Tepeyác, he once again saw the Holy Mother surrounded by the beauty of the heavenly lights.

(Juan Diego and the Holy Mother enter.)

Juan Diego:	O Holy Mother, I have failed you. The Bishop did not believe me. I knew I was not worthy. You should have chosen the *padre* from the village.
The Holy Mother:	Juan, do you not know that you are in my graces? I have chosen you and I will make this happen as it should.
Juan Diego:	But the Bishop has sent me away. He did not believe I have really seen you.

From *¡Teatro! Hispanic Plays for Young People*. Copyright © 1996. Teacher Ideas Press. (800) 237-6124.

| The Holy Mother: | Go back to the Bishop and give him my message again. A church must be built on this hill in my name. |
| Juan Diego: | Holy Mother, I will do as you ask. |

(*Both exit.*)

Scene 4: At the cathedral.

(*Brother Thomas and Sister Carmen enter.*)

Brother Thomas:	Here comes that Aztec man Juan Diego, again.
Sister Carmen:	I thought you told him not to come back.
Brother Thomas:	I did, but here he comes. I wonder what kind of holy mission he's on this time.

(*Juan Diego enters.*)

Juan Diego:	Please forgive me. I know you told me not to come back, but I must see the Bishop.
Brother Thomas:	You have already seen the Bishop.
Juan Diego:	But the Bishop didn't believe me, and I have been sent back to give him the message again.
Sister Carmen:	Sent back? Who sent you back?
Juan Diego:	The Holy Mother herself.
Brother Thomas:	The Bishop has already seen you, and he is too busy to see you again.
Juan Diego:	The Holy Mother has given me a message for the Bishop. It is very important that the Bishop believe this message.

(*The Bishop enters.*)

The Bishop:	Juan Diego, you have returned.
Juan Diego:	Please listen to me, Your Excellency. I am truly on a holy mission. I told the Holy Mother that you did not believe my word, and she said that a church must be built to her on the hill of Tepeyác. Your Excellency, I am not lying. A poor farmer like myself would never try to see the Bishop with a story like this if it were not true.
The Bishop:	But Juan, not many people get to see the Holy Mother.
Juan Diego:	But I did. On the hill of Tepeyác.

From *¡Teatro! Hispanic Plays for Young People.* Copyright © 1996. Teacher Ideas Press. (800) 237-6124.

Brother Thomas:	Your Excellency, I tried to tell him not to bother you again, but he returned, insisting on seeing you.
The Bishop:	Juan, your story is still too incredible to believe. It is not an easy task to build a shrine just because someone comes to me and tells me to build it.
Juan Diego:	I'm not telling you to build it. The Holy Mother is.
The Bishop:	Juan, if you have truly seen the Blessed Mother, bring me a sign that the miracle is real. If not, then never come to me with this story again. (*He exits.*)
Brother Thomas:	I told you not to come back and bother the Bishop. Now don't come back again unless you have a sign of the miracle.

(*All exit.*)

Scene 5: The hill of Tepeyác.

The Narrator:	On his way back to tell the Holy Mother that he needed a sign, Juan Diego received news that his uncle was dying. Juan rushed to his uncle's side, but when he arrived, it was almost too late. The family had already called the *padre* because the uncle knew he would not live another day. Juan rushed to tell the Holy Mother what had happened and to ask for forgiveness for not coming right back to her.

(*Juan Diego and the Holy Mother enter.*)

Juan Diego:	O Blessed Mother, I did not return from the cathedral because my uncle is dying and is not expected to last another day. We have called for the *padre* to come and say the last prayers. Also, I have failed in my holy mission again. The Bishop did not believe me this time either. He has asked that I bring back a sign that my vision of you is a true miracle. Please help me, Blessed Mother.
The Holy Mother:	Juan, do you not know that I am always here to help you? I have already cured your uncle. He will live many more years.
Juan Diego:	Blessed Mother, thank you. You are truly a gift sent to us from heaven.
The Holy Mother:	Now go to the top of the hill where only the cactus grows. There you will find a rosebush in bloom. Take those roses to the Bishop and he will believe. Take those roses to the Bishop and tell him to build the church in my honor.

(*Both exit.*)

The Narrator:	Juan Diego went to the top of the hill and there was a beautiful rosebush in full bloom. When Juan saw the roses blooming on that cold winter day, he knew it was the miracle he had asked for.

From ¡*Teatro! Hispanic Plays for Young People.* Copyright © 1996. Teacher Ideas Press. (800) 237-6124.

Scene 6: At the cathedral.

(*Brother Thomas and Sister Carmen enter.*)

Brother Thomas:	I don't believe it. Here comes Juan Diego.
Sister Carmen:	The Bishop himself told him not to come back.
Brother Thomas:	Well, I'm not letting him see the Bishop again.
Sister Carmen:	I would never bother the Bishop with the news that Juan Diego had returned for a third time.
Brother Thomas:	We'll just send him on his way until he gets the message to stop returning and bothering us.

(*Juan Diego enters, wearing his* tilma.)

Juan Diego:	I have come to see the Bishop.
Brother Thomas:	Juan Diego, you are a good man. Why do you keep bothering us like this?
Sister Carmen:	Didn't you hear the Bishop himself? He told you not to come back.
Juan Diego:	He told me to bring him proof of the miracle.
Brother Thomas:	Well, I don't see the Holy Mother around anywhere, so you might as well just go home.
Sister Carmen:	Please, Juan Diego, just go home.
Juan Diego:	But I have a sign from the Holy Mother. She has given me a sign to show to the Bishop.
Brother Thomas:	Juan Diego, no one believes that you have seen a miracle. We are not going to tell the Bishop you are here again.
Juan Diego:	But I do have the sign the Bishop asked for.
Brother Thomas:	If you have the sign, let us see it.
Sister Carmen:	Let us see the sign of the miracle. Then you will see the Bishop.

(*The characters act out the scene as the narrator speaks.*)

The Narrator:	Juan Diego opened his *tilma* and showed the roses to the Bishop's helpers. In their astonishment, they reached out to touch the roses. As they reached for the *tilma*, roses fell out of it. With great excitement they gathered the roses and called the Bishop.
Brother Thomas:	Your Excellency! Your Excellency!

From ¡*Teatro! Hispanic Plays for Young People.* Copyright © 1996. Teacher Ideas Press. (800) 237-6124.

Sister Carmen:	A miracle! Juan Diego has brought the miracle you asked for!
Brother Thomas:	He has brought roses in the winter!

(*The Bishop rushes in.*)

The Bishop:	What is it? What are you calling so excitedly for?
Brother Thomas:	Your Excellency, Juan Diego has returned.
Sister Carmen:	He has the sign you asked for.
The Bishop:	Is this true, Juan Diego?
Juan Diego:	The Blessed Mother has given me a sign to give to you. When you see this sign, you are to know that my vision of her is true, and you are to build a church dedicated to her. Then my holy mission will be completed.

(*The characters act out the scene as the narrator speaks.*)

The Narrator:	Juan Diego then opened his *tilma* and, when roses fell out of it, the Bishop knew Juan Diego was telling the truth. The Bishop picked up the roses and smelled their wonderful beauty. Even more miraculously, inside Juan Diego's *tilma* was the image of the Holy Mother, as Juan Diego had seen her on the hill of Tepeyác, surrounded by roses and the heavenly light. At the sight of the holy image, the Bishop and his helpers fell to their knees and prayed to the Holy Mother.
The Bishop:	It is a miracle. The Holy Mother has blessed us with this vision. We will build the church in her honor.

(*All exit.*)

The Narrator:	The Bishop built a church on the site Juan Diego showed him on the hill of Tepeyác. Now the site is called Guadalupe. To this day, Juan Diego's *tilma* with the image of the Holy Mother is kept inside the shrine to the Blessed Virgin. Prayerful worshipers can look at the *tilma* and be reminded of the love the Holy Mother has for her people. For all eternity, the shrine of Our Lady of Guadalupe is a reminder of the miraculous apparition that appeared to Juan Diego many years ago.

From *¡Teatro! Hispanic Plays for Young People.* Copyright © 1996. Teacher Ideas Press. (800) 237-6124.

La Flor de La Noche Buena
The Flower of the Holy Night

Introduction

La Flor de La Noche Buena is the miracle legend of how the poinsettia, the favorite decorative plant during the Christmas season, got its red leaves. Mexicans call the plant *La Flor de La Noche Buena*. The literal translation is "The Flower of the Good Night," with the *La Noche Buena* being "Christmas Eve."

The plant is native to Mexico, where it can grow as tall as ten feet, with leaves up to one foot in length. In the United States, it is the common, but smaller, potted plant that is a favorite holiday decoration. The Aztecs called the plant *Cuetlaxochitl*, "the flower of purity." The Spanish associated the plant with the Christmas season because the season is the plant's most colorful period.

The plant was introduced to the United States by Joel R. Poinsett. Poinsett was a botanist and legislator from South Carolina. He was the first United States ambassador to Mexico, from 1825 to 1830. Attracted to the plant and its colorful abundance, calling it "painted leaves," Poinsett took cuttings of it back to his plantation in South Carolina when he returned in 1830. Eventually, the plant became known as the poinsettia after Poinsett and its association with the Christmas season became even more defined in the United States. One reason for its acceptance as the Christmas plant is because of its traditional Christmas colors. Its green leaves came to symbolize the continuation of life, and its red leaves the blood shed by Christ.

La Flor de La Noche Buena is dramatically similar to another miracle story, *The Juggler of Notre Dame*. Both stories tell about how a young child discovers the true gift of love and, in doing so, accomplishes a miracle.

The story of *La Flor de La Noche Buena* occurs during the time of another Christmas tradition, *Las Posadas,* the nine-day celebration and reenactment of the journey of Mary and Joseph searching for lodging in Bethlehem. *Las Posadas*, translated as "the inns," originated in Spain during the Middle Ages. It was part of an annual cycle of plays used to teach Christian values. Mexican legend tells that the practice originated in the New World in the convent of San Aguatín de Acolmán near Mexico City. Fray Diego de Soria received permission from the Pope to celebrate nine *Misas de Aguinaldo*, or Gift Masses, from December 16th to December 24th. The masses were to celebrate the Holy Nativity.

Las Posadas are community celebrations that dramatize Mary and Joseph's search for lodging. Community members costumed as Mary and Joseph, accompanied by children dressed as angels and shepherds, lead the procession as it goes from house to house. For nine nights, the procession follows Mary and Joseph as they seek lodging. In the traditional *Las Posadas*, Lucifer would go from house to house for the first eight nights and persuade the owners of the house not to give lodging to Mary and Joseph. In this interpretation of Lucifer, he is not so much an evil character as a trickster. On the ninth night, Christmas Eve, Mary and Joseph finally receive lodging.

The families reenacting the journey would stop and sing at each house on each of the nine nights. On the ninth night, they all went to the final house and celebrated with food and song. The event has evolved into one that has Mary and Joseph finding lodging each of the nine nights. For each of the nine nights, families celebrate the Christmas season with food and good cheer in all the houses they go to.

Sometimes, communities will perform a condensed one-day version of *Las Posadas* as a preface to another story, *Los Pastores*, The Shepherd's Play. *Los Pastores* is a continuation of the biblical account of the birth of Christ, featuring the journey of the shepherds following the holy star over the manger to Bethlehem. *Los Pastores* is presented in the following play.

Communities in New Mexico also celebrate the Christmas season with *farolitos* and *luminarias*. In various parts of New Mexico, these terms have different meanings. Usually, *farolitos* are small paper bags with lit candles in them, which are placed around homes as holiday decorations. *Luminarias* are small bonfires. In my family, however, and in others in our community, we always called the paper bags with candles in them *luminarias*. To honor my own family's traditions, I have followed this practice in this play.

Staging

The play needs only simple interiors, represented by table and chairs.

Props

Two sets of angel wings	Sticks for making a god's eye
Star piñata	Colorful yarn for making a god's eye
Bags of candy	Paper bags
Bowls	Candles
Plates	A bag of sand
Napkins	A red-leafed poinsettia
A finished god's eye (see fig. 8 in the introduction to this book)	

Costumes

See figures 1, 2, and 8 in the introduction to this book.

Cast of Characters

The Narrator

The Martínez Family:

> Maria, *a young girl*
>
> Papa, *the father of Maria*
>
> Mama, *the mother of Maria*
>
> Theresa, *Maria's older sister*
>
> Carlito, *Maria's older brother*

The Priest

Scene 1: In a rural village at Maria's house.
Day One of Las Posadas.

(The scene opens with Maria watching her sister Theresa and brother Carlito getting dressed in their angel costumes.)

The Narrator:	At the Martínez house, Maria, the youngest in the Martínez family, is watching her sister and brother get dressed for day one of *Las Posadas*. This evening will be the first night of the nine processionals reenacting the journey of Joseph and Mary searching for lodging in Bethlehem.
Theresa:	*(Putting on her angel wings.)* Oh, look how wonderful they are.
Carlito:	I can't get mine on. I think they're too small.
Theresa:	Here, let me help you. *(She helps him with the wings, but they are too small.)* You know, I think they are too small. Are you sure these are yours?
Carlito:	I think they are. These are the ones Mama gave me.
Theresa:	Let's try again. *(They try to put on the wings for a second time, but they still don't fit.)* I don't think they are going to go on. I think you have the wrong wings. You must have the wings for one of the smaller children.
Carlito:	But these are the only wings Mama gave me.
Theresa:	Well, they're too small.
Maria:	Maybe they will fit me. I can be one of the angels this year!
Theresa:	Maria, one day you will get to be one of the angels, but this year we get to be the angels.
Maria:	That's not fair. I'm old enough to be one of the angels.
Carlito:	I had to wait to be one of the angels in the *Las Posadas* procession. Every year, the procession would start and I would be so jealous of the kids who got to be the angels.
Theresa:	It's a special honor to be one of the angels who go with the shepherds with Joseph and Mary.
Carlito:	Mama said the angels are closest to Baby Jesus. I think it's the best part of the procession.
Maria:	That's why I want to be one of the angels.
Carlito:	Maria, you have to wait until you're a little bigger, just like I did.
Maria:	But those wings are for a younger person like me. They don't fit someone as old as you.

From *¡Teatro! Hispanic Plays for Young People*. Copyright © 1996. Teacher Ideas Press. (800) 237-6124.

Carlito:	They are for a smaller person, not a younger person. There's a difference, you know.
Maria:	Even you get to be in the procession. You get to be an angel!
Carlito:	But Mama already said you could go with the singers. Besides, it wouldn't work if all the kids were angels.
Theresa:	Some kids have to be the singers.
Maria:	But being a singer isn't any fun. The singers are the adults. The kids just walk in the procession carrying candles.
Theresa:	That's not true. If you know the words, you can sing. And a lot of the adults carry candles.
Maria:	But I don't know the words. I can't sing along.
Carlito:	But that is how you learn the words. Just sing along this year and you'll be okay.
Theresa:	Just be happy you get to go on the procession. Sometimes, if you are too small, you have to stay home.
Maria:	Not really. When I was small, Papa would carry me. You guys don't get the point. I want to be an angel this year.
Carlito:	You don't get the point. Mama only brought over two pairs of wings. One for me and one for Theresa.
Theresa:	Maybe next year you can be an angel.
Maria:	But you yourself said the wings are too small. They could fit me.
Carlito:	No, they just seem too small. I think they will actually fit. (*He struggles to put on the wings and finally succeeds in getting them on.*)
Theresa:	Maria, really you can be an angel next year.
Maria:	But I want to be something special for Baby Jesus, too.
Theresa:	You will be. You'll be the best candle holder and the best singer.
Carlito:	And you'll be in the procession.
Theresa:	That's a good-enough gift.
Maria:	But I wanted to give something really special this year.
Carlito:	You will. It's only the first night of *Las Posadas*.
Maria:	But still, being an angel is better.

From *¡Teatro! Hispanic Plays for Young People.* Copyright © 1996. Teacher Ideas Press. (800) 237-6124.

Theresa: | Maybe next year. Now let's go. The procession is starting.

(*Theresa and Carlito now have on their angel costumes. All exit.*)

Scene 2: *Day three of* Las Posadas.

The Narrator: | Day three of *Las Posadas*.

(*Papa and Mama enter, with a large star piñata. During this scene, the family fills the piñata.*)

Papa: | This is a great piñata! When I was a small boy, we always had just these little piñatas. Nowadays the piñatas are so much bigger. Everyone told me, "Make it extra big." So I did.

Mama: | Kids! It's time to fill the piñata.

(*Theresa, Carlito, and Maria enter, running.*)

Theresa: | This is my favorite part of *Las Posadas*.

Carlito: | Mine too!

Maria: | After the procession, we get to have a party and break the piñata!

Papa: | This year we have to bring the piñata. Now I made this one extra big and the ladies from the church took a collection and we were able to buy all this stuff to put in it.

Maria: | (*Excitedly.*) What did you get?

Carlito: | What are we going to put in the piñata this year?

Papa: | (*Showing them bags of candy.*) Candy!

Mama: | So let's get started. Your father made it, but it's your job to fill it. And don't take too long, because we need to get ready for tonight's procession.

(*During the rest of this scene, the family fills the piñata.*)

Theresa: | Let's hope Maria doesn't mope all through this one like she did last night.

Papa: | Maria, were you moping?

Theresa: | Oh, she's still sulking because she can't be an angel this year.

Maria: | I'm not sulking. I just thought it would be a special gift to Baby Jesus if I could be an angel in the procession.

Mama: | Oh Maria, just being in the procession is a good-enough gift. Baby Jesus sees you walking in the procession, and that's good enough.

From *¡Teatro! Hispanic Plays for Young People*. Copyright © 1996. Teacher Ideas Press. (800) 237-6124.

Carlito:	See, I told you.
Maria:	But I want to do something even more special.
Papa:	Like what, *jita*.
Maria:	Like be an angel. Like lead the procession. Like bring special gifts to the church.
Papa:	I can understand that. I've always wanted to play Lucifer.
Carlito:	You would be "El Diablo!"
Papa:	It's the best part. You get to run ahead of the procession and be at the house when everybody arrives. And then you get to convince the people at the house not to let Mary and Joseph have a place to sleep. (*He stands up and, with exaggerated drama, does a speech from the part.*) "Do not let them stay. They might be common thieves. And besides, the inn is full. There is no room. Go look somewhere else."
Maria:	But Papa that is doing the Devil's work.
Papa:	But the part is important to the story because only by defeating the devil on the final night do we tell the beautiful story of Mary and Joseph. So see, Maria, there is something I've always wanted to do to but I have had to be happy with just being a singer in the procession.
Maria:	But you are doing something special. You got to make the piñata. That's a special gift.
Papa:	I never thought of it that way. I guess anything you do for *Las Posadas* can be a special gift. I just thought I was making the piñata.
Theresa:	See, Maria, anything you do, even just walking in the procession, is a special gift.
Maria:	(*Not convinced.*) I guess so.
Carlito:	How come you made a star, Papa? Last year, someone made a donkey because it was supposed to be one of the shepherds' donkeys.
Papa:	I thought I would make something more special than a donkey. You can have a donkey piñata any day of the year. But only at this time of year can you have a piñata like this. This isn't just any old star. This is the star of Bethlehem, which shines over the manger.
Theresa:	That's a great idea, Papa!
Papa:	I thought so.
Maria:	See, you did do something special. That's what I want to do.

From ¡*Teatro! Hispanic Plays for Young People.* Copyright © 1996. Teacher Ideas Press. (800) 237-6124.

Papa:	Don't worry so much, Maria. When you get a little older, you will.
Mama:	Time to go. The procession is starting. Is the piñata all filled up?
Carlito:	Just a few more pieces, Mama.

(*The girls put the last pieces of candy into the piñata and close it up.*)

Papa:	Good job, kids. Let's give it a test before we go. Theresa, turn your sister around and Maria, close your eyes.

(*Papa holds up the piñata. Theresa turns Maria around three times and points her at the piñata. Maria tries to hit the piñata three times but Papa pulls the piñata away each time. All laugh with each of Maria's swings.*)

Papa:	Good. It's working. Everyone, let's go. And be careful with the piñata! We don't want it breaking early.
Carlito:	Papa, let me be the one to break the piñata!
Papa:	We'll see. Now let's go or we'll be late.

(*All exit.*)

Scene 3: Day five of Las Posadas.

The Narrator:	Day five of *Las Posadas.*

(*Theresa, Maria, and Carlito enter. They begin setting the table for a feast.*)

Theresa:	Here, Carlito, take these bowls and put them on the table.
Theresa:	Tonight the procession ends at our house. Maria, make sure that the napkins are arranged in a special way. We can't have them just in a pile like we usually do.
Maria:	I'm trying to put them into the shape of a star. For the star of Bethlehem.
Theresa:	That's a good idea!
Maria:	I got the idea from the piñata Papa made. I'm trying to do a special job.
Carlito:	Don't you wish we had the piñata every night?
Theresa:	I do.
Maria:	So do I.
Theresa:	This year you were almost the one who broke it.
Maria:	Papa kept pulling it up too high. I couldn't reach it.

From *¡Teatro! Hispanic Plays for Young People.* Copyright © 1996. Teacher Ideas Press. (800) 237-6124.

Carlito:	He wouldn't even let me hit it.
Theresa:	He told me it wouldn't look right if he let his own kids break the piñata.
Carlito:	That's not fair! We should get a fair chance just like everybody else.
Theresa:	But I like not being the one who breaks it. Then you can get to the candy faster when it all falls on the ground.
Carlito:	But still, a couple of hits would have been all right.
Maria:	I got a couple of hits.
Carlito:	That's because you're the littlest. He's always doing you favors.
Maria:	No, I really hit it on my own!
Theresa:	Oh you two, stop it. We all had fun and got some candy, and that's all that really counts anyway. Now both of you, smell the air.

(*Carlito and Maria together take a big sniff of the air.*)

Theresa:	Doesn't it smell good! Mama has been cooking all day long.
Maria:	It smells so good.
Theresa:	*Biscochitos*!
Carlito:	My favorite cookies!
Theresa:	*Sopaipillas*!
Maria:	With honey and powered sugar!
Theresa:	*Empanaditas*! *Posole*!
Carlito:	Our favorite Christmas foods! I wish she cooked like this all year long.
Maria:	Yeah, how come she doesn't?
Theresa:	This is her special Christmas cooking.
Carlito:	She told me she learned how to cook all this food from *abuelita* when she was growing up. Grandma used to make all this special food at Christmas time, too.
Maria:	See, that's just what I mean. It seems like everybody does something special for Baby Jesus except for me.
Theresa:	That's not true, Maria.
Maria:	Yes it is. You both get to be angels. Papa made the piñata. Mama makes special food for everybody. I don't do anything special.

From ¡*Teatro! Hispanic Plays for Young People*. Copyright © 1996. Teacher Ideas Press. (800) 237-6124.

Theresa:	Maria, you're going to ruin *Las Posadas* for everybody if you don't stop worrying about having to do something special. Sometimes you just can't do anything special and that's just all there is to it.
Carlito:	You're too little anyway.
Maria:	But I don't want to be too little.
Theresa:	Look, here is an idea. You know how on the last night of *Las Posadas* the procession ends at the church.
Carlito:	You know, on *La Noche Buena*, Christmas Eve.
Theresa:	Well this year you are old enough to stay up for midnight mass. On *La Noche Buena*, all the children usually bring gifts to the church for Baby Jesus to celebrate his birth. You can bring something as a gift.
Maria:	Like what?
Theresa:	Here, let me show you. (*She gets out a god's eye weaving.*) See, this year I made a god's eye with some of my favorite yarn.
Maria:	What did you make, Carlito?
Carlito:	Nothing yet. But I'm going to make some *papel picado*. I have some special paper left over from *El Día de Los Muertos* when we made the *ofrenda*.
Theresa:	I'll help you make a god's eye. I have a lot of yarn left over, and we can make a really colorful one.
Maria:	Okay, but I wanted to make a special gift of my own. It'll just seem like I copied yours.
Theresa:	Maria, you're not helping out very much here.
Maria:	I'm trying to. I really am. Everyone is always telling me that I'm too little, but I don't think so. I really want to give Baby Jesus a special gift this year.
Theresa:	Well *La Noche Buena* is just a few days away, so if you want to make one of my god's eyes, we better get started pretty soon. Now let's finish up here. We have to have everything finished by the time the procession starts. It ends at our house tonight, and Mama wants all the food to be really special when everyone gets here.

(*All exit.*)

From *¡Teatro! Hispanic Plays for Young People.* Copyright © 1996. Teacher Ideas Press. (800) 237-6124.

Scene 4: Day nine of Las Posadas, La Noche Buena.

| The Narrator: | Day nine of *Las Posadas*, *La Noche Buena*, Christmas Eve. |

(The Martínez family enters. The parents are carrying paper bags, candles, and a box of sand. During this scene, the family, except for Maria, makes luminarias *by filling the bags with sand and putting a candle in each one. Maria is carrying a bag of yarn and a god's eye she is trying to make.)*

Papa:	I can't believe it's *La Noche Buena* already. *Las Posadas* seemed to go by so fast his year.
Theresa:	Every single night was fun this year. The processions, the singing.
Carlito:	The piñata.
Papa:	The food.
Mama:	All of you, let's not forget why we do *Las Posadas*. It's not just for the fiesta. Remember, it's to prepare for *La Noche Buena*. To remind us of the journey of Mary and Joseph looking for a place to stay so we could have *La Noche Buena*.
Theresa:	Maybe next year I can be Mary in the procession.
Carlito:	And I could be Joseph!
Mama:	Theresa, you are almost old enough to be Mary, but Carlito, you will need a few more years to be Joseph.
Papa:	And don't forget that every other kid in the village wants to be Mary and Joseph.
Theresa:	(*Complaining*.) And we can't be playing favorites and have your kids be Mary and Joseph can we? Just like the piñata.
Papa:	Now don't bring up the piñata again. I did the right thing that night.
Carlito:	Not for us.
Papa:	But for the other kids, I did.
Mama:	Oh you all, stop it. It's *La Noche Buena*. This is my favorite night of the year. You kids help your father and me make the *luminarias*. And be careful not to spill any of the sand on the floor.
Theresa:	I just love how the *luminarias* look when we come back from church. All the candles shining through the bags. All the bags lining the path to the house. They're like little stars leading us home.
Carlito:	Like the star of Bethlehem. Only a lot of them.

From *¡Teatro! Hispanic Plays for Young People*. Copyright © 1996. Teacher Ideas Press. (800) 237-6124.

Papa:	I never thought of it like that before. That's a very good idea, Carlito.
Carlito:	Are we going to put them around the top of the house this year Papa?
Papa:	Of course. It's tradition!
Mama:	Maria, what are you doing so quietly over there. Come and help us make *luminarias.*
Maria:	I'm trying to make a god's eye for my present for Baby Jesus.
Mama:	Let me see how it's looking.
Maria:	Not yet. I'm not finished yet.
Carlito:	I have my *papel picado* all cut out. I made them all stars for—
Theresa:	We know already. For the "star of Bethlehem."
Carlito:	Don't make fun of me. It's my present to the Baby Jesus.
Theresa:	I'm not making fun. It's just that for this *Las Posadas*, all I'm going to remember about you is the star of Bethlehem.
Mama:	Theresa, leave your brother alone. If you want to be Mary next year, you'll have to be better to your little brother.
Theresa:	Doesn't it count that I helped Maria get her present for Baby Jesus together. I gave her the idea and taught her how to do it.
Maria:	Not very well. The yarn keeps falling off the sticks.
Theresa:	Here, let me see. (*She goes over to Maria and inspects the god's eye she has been making.*) I don't think you are wrapping the yarn around tight enough.
Maria:	I'm doing it just like you showed me how to.
Theresa:	Let me show you again. (*She takes the god's eye and wraps the yarn around it again.*) See, just like this. Wrap the yarn tight, so it stays on, but not too tight, or it doesn't look right.
Maria:	It's easy for you because you've made a lot of them.
Theresa:	That's true. But you can do this. You're not too little.
Maria:	(*Frustrated.*) I can't do it.
Mama:	Yes you can, Maria. Just keep trying. You'll get it.
Maria:	But I can't! Every time I try, it all falls apart.
Theresa:	Then let me try to finish it for you.

From *¡Teatro! Hispanic Plays for Young People.* Copyright © 1996. Teacher Ideas Press. (800) 237-6124.

Maria:	But if you finish it, then the god's eye will be your present, not mine.
Papa:	It'll be your present, Maria. You did most of the work.
Carlito:	Papa helped me with the *papel picado*. I was having trouble with making the cuts look right, and he had to help me with a lot of them.
Mama:	See, Maria, it's okay to get help.
Maria:	I know, but what is happening is what I was afraid would happen. I'm not going to have my own special present for Baby Jesus.
Mama:	But Maria, that's all right. Baby Jesus will know that you wanted to give him a special present.
Maria:	But you always have told me that the spirit of *La Noche Buena* is about giving presents, not just getting presents. And now that I'm old enough to go to midnight mass, I want to bring the most special present in the whole world for Baby Jesus.
Papa:	(*Looking at his watch.*) Midnight mass! It's almost time for *La Misa del Gallo*! We've spent the whole evening making *luminarias* and now it's time, it's time to go on the final procession of *Las Posadas*.
Maria:	But I'm not finished with my god's eye.
Papa:	But *jita*, it's time to go.
Maria:	Then I'm not going on the procession. I'm going to stay here and finish the god's eye.
Mama:	Maria, I know you want to finish the god's eye, but it's time to go. Maybe you can finish it tomorrow and take it over then.
Papa:	Right now, we need to get all these *luminarias* around the house and lit before we go. I'll need all of your help.
Theresa:	Can I light them, Papa?
Carlito:	Me too?
Papa:	You can light the ones on the ground, but I'll light the ones on the house.
Maria:	(*Very disappointed.*) My god's eye came unraveled again. I guess I'm not supposed to have a present for Baby Jesus this year.
Mama:	That's okay, Maria. Baby Jesus knows you tried to have a present.
Papa:	Time to go. Everyone grab some *luminarias*.

(*All exit carrying the luminarias they made. Maria exits dejectedly.*)

From *¡Teatro! Hispanic Plays for Young People*. Copyright © 1996. Teacher Ideas Press. (800) 237-6124.

Scene 5: At the church.

The Narrator: | At the end of the nine days of *Las Posadas*, Mary and Joseph finally find lodging. After the traditional late-night dinner, the families bring an end to *La Noche Buena* with a final procession to the church for midnight mass.

(*The Martínez Family, except for Maria, enters and sits before the priest.*)

The Priest: | Welcome to the most holy night of the year, *La Noche Buena*. Before we begin the holy mass, let's have the children bring up their presents for the Baby Jesus.

(*Theresa and Carlito give their presents to the priest.*)

Papa: | Where is Maria?

Mama: | She was right behind us in the procession. I thought she was with you.

Papa: | Theresa, do you know where your sister is?

Theresa: | I thought she was just behind us.

Carlito: | She told me she couldn't come without a present for Baby Jesus.

Papa: | She didn't go back home, did she?

Carlito: | I don't know. She just took off right as we went past the field. I'll go look for her. (*He runs out.*)

Mama: | I'm worried. It's too late for a little girl to be wandering in the fields.

Papa: | I'll go look for her . . .

(*As he gets up to go look for her, Maria comes into the church. She is holding something behind her back.*)

Mama: | Maria, where have you been!

Papa: | This isn't right, Maria. We thought you were old enough to come to midnight mass, not run off and hide in the fields.

Maria: | I was getting a present.

Mama: | You were what?

Maria: | I was getting a present for Baby Jesus.

Papa: | In the field?

From *¡Teatro! Hispanic Plays for Young People*. Copyright © 1996. Teacher Ideas Press. (800) 237-6124.

Maria:	I couldn't come to midnight mass with nothing. I love Baby Jesus too much. So I went into the field to wait until mass was over. When I walked by these plants, they turned this beautiful color. So I brought them as a present for Baby Jesus. (*She takes a bright red poinsettia out from behind her back and gives it to the priest.*)
The Priest:	Maria, where did you get this plant?
Maria:	From the field by the church, *padre*.
The Priest:	This is the plant that grows wild in the field. It is most abundant at this time of year. But its leaves have never been red. They are always green.
Maria:	They turned red when I walked by them thinking about Baby Jesus. They were so beautiful I brought one for my special present.

(*Carlito runs in.*)

Carlito:	Mama! Papa! You should see it. The whole field is filled with red plants. Just like the ones Maria has. Come and see them. They're beautiful!
The Priest:	*¡Un milagro!* The child's love has brought us a miracle for *La Noche Buena*.

(*All rush out, talking about the miracle.*)

The Narrator:	And from that time on, the poinsettia has given us its red leaves on *La Noche Buena* to remind us that the best gift of all is a heart full of love.

From *¡Teatro! Hispanic Plays for Young People.* Copyright © 1996. Teacher Ideas Press. (800) 237-6124.

Los Pastores
The Shepherds

Introduction

Los Pastores, The Shepherds, is the most well-known and popular Nativity play in the Hispanic Southwest. A descendant of the Medieval religious plays of Europe, it is the Biblical story of the birth of Christ. These liturgical dramas have existed in Europe since the ninth century. The Nativity play was an established part of Spain's dramatic literature during Spain's Golden Age. Lope de Vega's *Los Pastores de Belén* is one of the primary examples of the well-developed genre of Spanish Nativity plays.

Dr. Juan B. Rael, Professor Emeritus of Spanish at Stanford University, has traced the origins and development of Nativity plays in the New World. His studies have revealed that the plays were probably written by Franciscan missionaries in Mexico, and that these plays were based on European models. The Franciscans and other settlers carried these plays from the interior of Mexico to its northern provinces.

The traditional performance of *Los Pastores* was usually preceded by a presentation of *Las Posadas*. *Las Posadas,* presented in the previous play of this book, *La Flor de La Noche Buena,* is a community reenactment of Mary and Joseph's nine-day search for lodging in Bethlehem. When performed in conjunction with *Los Pastores*, however, it is condensed to a one-day event. It then becomes a preface to the second part of the Nativity story, the birth of Christ, which is the subject of *Los Pastores*.

Los Pastores is traditionally comprised of both songs and recitations. The songs are a mixture of several traditional and formal Spanish musical styles. In addition, the language of the recitations has been described by Professor Rael as the formal language of educated Spaniards, not the common Spanish spoken in the Hispanic Southwest.

Part of a larger dramatic experience of Spanish colonialists that included plays about Adam and Eve, the appearances of the Virgin of Guadalupe, and historical secular dramas, performances of *Los Pastores* were church-sponsored community events. Scripts were passed from community to community and generation to generation. Often roles were passed down within families.

Not only did *Los Pastores* present the Biblical events of Christ's birth, but it was also an enormously popular and entertaining play about the eternal struggle between good and evil, and humanity's efforts to resist temptation. While its central theme and events are serious and religious, the play's great popularity is also because of the comedy, fun, and irreverence, similar to the *Second Shepherd's Play* of the Wakefield cycle in Britain, woven into the play. Several of the play's characters are buffoons tricked by temptation, and several of its scenes are almost slapstick in nature. The roles of Lucifer and the buffoons were often the most coveted because of their potential for outlandish portrayal. Traditional performances are also marked by ad-libs that poked fun at members of the community.

One of the lines of the play has become a well-known and often-repeated *dicho,* or folk proverb, used whenever someone does not want to do something he or she has been asked to do. The line is: "*Si quiere la gloria verme, que venga la gloria acá.*" "If 'glory' wants to see me, let glory come to me." The line is spoken by an especially lazy shepherd.

This version of *Los Pastores* is based upon several traditional versions. Though language and plot have been simplified for purposes of this adaptation, it contains all the primary characters and all the essential dramatic and textual elements of the full, traditional version. Also, verses that originally were meant to be sung have been translated to dramatic speech. The characters' names are from the traditional versions.

Staging

This play takes place outdoors. A clear, open space is best to indicate the exterior scenes of this play.

Props

Shepherd's crooks	Small cradle
Two swords	A book of prayers
A sheepskin	Crystals and jewels
A woolen fleece	A bag of *tortillas*
Small altar cloth	Blankets
A honeycomb	Two guitars

Costumes

See figures 1, 2, 7, and 8 in the introduction to this book.

Cast of Characters

The Narrator

The Hermit, *full of missionary spirit, a God-fearing shepherd*

The Shepherds:

Gila, *a young shepherdess*

Bartolo, *a lazy shepherd*

Bato, *leader of the shepherds*

Tubal

Tebano

Lépido

Tetuán

Gil

An angel

Lucifer, *an outcast angel who wants to conquer the world*

The Archangel Miguel, *representing the good in humanity*

Scene 1: A field outside of Bethlehem on **La Noche Buena,** *Christmas Eve.*

(The Shepherds are in the field watching their flock.)

Bato:	What a beautiful night
Tubal:	Just look at the stars. They've never been so bright!
Lépido:	Everything is so calm and peaceful. It must have been an evening like this when God created the world.
Gil:	Even the sheep are especially peaceful tonight.
Bato:	Bartolo! Wake up. You are so lazy you are going to miss the most beautiful night of the year.
Bartolo:	I'm too tired. Let me sleep some more.
Bato:	Gila, shake Bartolo. He's been sleeping all day.
Gila:	*(She gives Bartolo a shake.)* He won't wake up. He's too lazy.

(Tetuán enters, running excitedly.)

Tetuán:	*¡Pastores!* I was in the fields watching the sheep and I saw the most amazing sight. In the east a star . . . a bright star suddenly appeared.
Gila:	Tonight is a special night. All the stars have never looked so bright before.
Bato:	It's as if this were the most peaceful night since the beginning of creation.
Tetuán:	While I was watching the sheep, I was gazing at the heavenly sky, and I had the same feelings. But this isn't an ordinary star. It just suddenly burst into the sky. It was brighter than all the other stars in the sky. Even the little lambs took notice.
Bato:	You've been out with the sheep too long.
Gila:	It's time you come in and one of us will go out now.
Tetuán:	No, believe me *pastores.* It is a new star never in the sky before. Brighter, more beautiful. And then I heard the most beautiful singing. Almost like the heavens themselves were singing.
Bato:	Maybe it was Bartolo's snoring.

(All laugh.)

Tetuán:	No, that would have set the lambs running.

(All laugh and poke Bartolo, but he continues to sleep.)

From *¡Teatro! Hispanic Plays for Young People.* Copyright © 1996. Teacher Ideas Press. (800) 237-6124.

Tetuán:	This was a sound . . . well almost like the sound I'm hearing right now.
Bato:	It sounds like the voices of the heavenly angels and it seems that one of them is coming through these fields to us right now.

(As the Shepherds look around to identify the source of the sound, an Angel enters. When they see the Angel, they are shocked and frightened.)

Angel:	Shepherds, do not be frightened, because I bring good news. I have come to announce to you that the Christ is born. The greatest joy that the world has ever known has arrived tonight. I will tell you the story of the birth of the Christ child. When in the east the sun rose, Our Lady the Virgin was traveling. What pleasure and what joy there was for the blessed queen of the heavens. The weary travelers came to a *posada* and asked for shelter for the night. The innkeeper, sticking his head through the window, replied with an evil grace, "For him who has money my house is ready. For him who has no money, let God help him." The weary travelers continued to seek lodging until at last they found a night's rest.
Gila:	Tell us where he is.
Angel:	In *Belén* he is born. In a little shelter, swaddled in straw, where an ox and a mule adore the newborn Christ. The angels themselves sing to announce the coming of the Blessed Child.
Tetuán:	I heard the heavenly music. That was the music I heard in the fields.
Angel:	Shepherds of the earth, I was sent by God to let you know that the Messiah is born, the One foretold by the prophets. I am an ambassador from the celestial kingdom sent to give you this announcement.
Gila:	How beautiful this night is when Jesus was born and the angels sang along until it was dawn.
Angel:	*Pastores*, go on to *Belén* and give praise yourself to this great miracle.
Tebano:	We have heard the heavenly voices singing Glory to God in the highest, and peace on earth. Through the sweet air the wind carries the angels' voices with the many joyful songs they sing. Through the sweet air they are singing Glory to God in the highest.
Lépido:	Even the little lambs are happy and joyful tonight.
Gila:	*Pastores*, the time has arrived when we all will be traveling to the shelter in *Belén* to see the happy miracle. Gather our belongings and then with great pleasure we will begin our journey without any further loss of time.
Bato:	My brother *pastores*, Gila has spoken well. Let us go walking through these fields of flowers and let us travel happily that we may see the Messiah who was born on straw.

From *¡Teatro! Hispanic Plays for Young People*. Copyright © 1996. Teacher Ideas Press. (800) 237-6124.

| Gila: | Bartolo, get up! This is no time to sleep. Let us go and adore this Child born in *Belén*. |
| Angel: | The star will lead you to the Holy Child. A most brilliant star will guide you to Him who with purest love is the Redeemer of mankind. |

(*All gather their belongings and exit, excitedly talking about the Angel's news.*)

Scene 2: In a field outside a hermit's cave.

(*The Hermit enters and begins praying.*)

| The Hermit: | I pray to the true God to deliver me from temptation and evil. The devils try to tempt me, but I turn my sights to heaven and, with the sign of the cross I pray to the Heavenly Father. I pray all alone in my cave without any company other than the mice and insects. To my despair, I am becoming more tired and I cannot find anyone around here who can tell me if the Messiah whom the prophets announced in their holy prophecies is born. But who comes by my lonely cave so far from the paths of regular travelers? They are *pastores*. Perhaps they can tell me news of the Messiah. *¡Pastores! ¡Pastores!* |

(*The Shepherds enter.*)

Bato:	Who is that calling us?
Gila:	It looks like some lost soul who lives alone in these hills.
The Hermit:	Do not fear me, *pastores*. I am your servant, the hermit. Forgive me, but I seek news of the Messiah. I have lived alone in these caves for thirty years, living a life of prayer and penance, and still the heavens have not sent me news of the Messiah who was prophesied.
Gila:	Good hermit, tonight we have heard the news.
Bato:	An angel came to us.
Tetuán:	I heard the heavenly voices singing while I tended to the sheep in the fields. Then I saw the Star of *Belén*.
Gil:	The Messiah is born in *Belén*.
The Hermit:	My prayers of thirty years have been answered!
Bato:	We are traveling to *Belén* to give praise to the Holy Child.
The Hermit:	*Pastores*, may I travel with you?
Bato:	Yes, you are welcome to travel to *Belén* with us.

From *¡Teatro! Hispanic Plays for Young People*. Copyright © 1996. Teacher Ideas Press. (800) 237-6124.

The Hermit:	Thank you, good *pastores*. But please be so kind as to give me something to eat. My life in the cave is a very simple one dedicated to prayer, and it has been days since I have had anything to eat. I am almost dead with hunger.
Bato:	Stay here with us as we rest from our journey. You are welcome to share our food with us. *Pastores*, we each have our duties to perform. Tubal, go to the mountains and get wood. Gil, bed down the flocks. Tebano and I will stay and play the guitars.
Gila:	(*Shaking Bartolo, who is already sleeping.*) Bartolo, bring the dishes, and I will serve the meat.
Bartolo:	I was just settling in for a fine rest and you come and bother me. But now that you mention it, I am hungry. Is there anything for a snack? If not, just give me the jug, because I am thirsty and I need a drink.
Gila:	Bartolo, you need to help.
Bartolo:	I won't help with any jobs because I am very tired and lazy today. And now I'm going to go back to my nap. Wake me when the food is ready.
Gila:	If you go to sleep, you will get nothing to eat.
Bartolo:	You will not let me sleep through the meal. We have traveled together too long and too far for you to treat Bartolo like that. For now, Gila, my dearest child, sleep overcomes me, and you know I suffer from colossal laziness. Just give me a nudge when the food is ready. (*He rolls over and goes to sleep.*)
Gila:	What am I going to do about Bartolo?
Bato:	He wants to sleep. Let him sleep. (*As he speaks, Gila gives* tortillas *to the shepherds. They eat the* tortillas *as the scene continues.*)
Lépido:	This night really is *La Noche Buena*, the good night we have been waiting for.
Tebano:	It is a night full of joy and love.
Bato:	The angels sing glory and peace to the newborn Child.
Gila:	The heavens, the earth, and the waters sing glory to God.
The Hermit:	For thirty years I have prayed and waited for this night. The earth is filled from the heavens to the ground with God's love. *Pastores*, thank you for allowing me to join you on your holy journey to *Belén*. And Gila, these *tortillas* are a gift from heaven for a hungry man such as myself.
Tebano:	You are right, hermit. These tortillas are a gift from the heavens.

From *¡Teatro! Hispanic Plays for Young People*. Copyright © 1996. Teacher Ideas Press. (800) 237-6124.

Bartolo:	(*Waking up and looking around.*) Hey! How come no one woke me up to eat.
Gila:	You wanted to sleep, so we let you sleep.
Bartolo:	But you know how much I like eating.
Gila:	We all know nobody can beat you when it comes to eating and sleeping. You are the best at both. But you are the worst when it comes to working.
Bartolo:	You are so mean! Why are you scolding me so much? How have I offended you? And why didn't you wake me to eat?
Gila:	Because you are so lazy. If you don't want to come to the meal, I am not going to bring it to you.
Bartolo:	But I am here now to see what is for dinner.
Gila:	The meal has come and gone.
Bartolo:	Oh why am I so cursed with laziness? Now I have missed dinner.
Bato:	(*Looking around.*) *Pastores*, it is beginning to snow.
Gila:	Even the sky is in amazement at the beauty of this holy night.
Bato:	*Pastores*, this heavenly snow will be our blankets tonight as we sleep. Let us sing praises to the blessed heavens, for tomorrow our journey will take us to *Belén* and we will see the Messiah.

(*The Shepherds wrap themselves in blankets and go to sleep.*)

Scene 3: Later in the night, as the shepherds sleep.

(*Lucifer enters and finds the Shepherds and the Hermit.*)

Lucifer:	I come to this earth from the deepest infernal caverns. My legions have brought news to me that on this fatal night the Messiah is born. I have come out troubled and astonished to find the angels singing in the heavens. If the Messiah is truly born, then my reign on earth will come to an end. But I will bring my wrath down upon this earth, and I will use my force in order that I may destroy the power of the Messiah. And these shepherds asleep here will die before they learn of the redemption. I will let the world be filled with vices of hatred and cries of suffering. I have ready seven deadly sins to make mortals fall into deadly crimes. The first is Pride. This sin will reign in men who have acquired honors, riches, and high office. The second is that cruel vice Greed. It will incite men to be mad before money and their desire for more of it. The third deadly vice will be Lust. It will kill virtue, trust, and honor among men and women alike. The next is

From *¡Teatro! Hispanic Plays for Young People.* Copyright © 1996. Teacher Ideas Press. (800) 237-6124.

Anger, which will cause a blindness that will sow war and hostility throughout the world. The fifth shall be Gluttony. It will be the sin of unrestrained pleasure and disorderly appetite. The sixth is Envy. Its destructive fire will burn in the hearts of men and set them against family and friend. Finally, the seventh vice will be Sloth. None shall escape its dangers as they fall into an eternal laziness, passing the days with nothing but sleep. Without any rest or truce, I vow eternal battle against this Redeemer. To this battle we will all go without fear. And if it is not possible to keep the Divine Word from bring born, then I will begin my war here with these sleeping shepherds, and I will use my skill to tempt these helpless shepherds. I will disguise myself and see if this Messiah is truly born. (*He approaches the sleeping hermit and wakes him.*) *Señor,* I am a weary traveler in the world, as you are. I am seeking news about a Messiah.

The Hermit:	It is true. The Messiah is born. We are on a holy journey to *Belén* to give praise to the Christ Child. You are welcome to accompany us so that you may give praise, too.
Lucifer:	That is one thing I am unable to do. But I will give you good advice to save you troubles on your own journey.
The Hermit:	What kind of trouble could there be on such a holy night as this?
Lucifer:	There will be cold and snow. Ferocious beasts lie ahead. But if you come with me to my country, there will be riches beyond imagination. Crystals, jewels.
The Hermit:	Go away with your stories of richness. We are on a journey to give glory to the greatest richness on earth.
Lucifer:	I have come to warn you about these false lies of a miracle birth in *Belén.*
The Hermit:	They are not lies, for the child born is the true Messiah.
Lucifer:	(*Aside to himself.*) Cursed be this hermit. His faith is an example of what will happen if all learn of this Messiah. I shall use all my powers to see if I can trap this hermit in my snares. He will be the first to fall to my seven deadly sins. (*To the hermit.*) Come with me away from these sleeping shepherds. Let's go over to the trees over there and we can speak more guardedly.

(*Lucifer takes the hermit to the side of the stage.*)

The Hermit:	Why do we have to go so far?
Lucifer:	Because your companions will hear us.
The Hermit:	But they are sleeping and dreaming.
Lucifer:	But now we will be able to talk more freely.

From *¡Teatro! Hispanic Plays for Young People.* Copyright © 1996. Teacher Ideas Press. (800) 237-6124.

The Hermit:	Then begin. I am listening.
Lucifer:	Please listen and consider my words. I am the most powerful man there is in the world. There is not a book in the world I have not studied. I have seen the greatest secrets of the world. I have witnessed miracles. I have the power to see into men's souls.
The Hermit:	That truly is a great power.
Lucifer:	Confess then. I have seen you looking at the shepherdess sleeping over there.
The Hermit:	Shhh! Speak more quietly. I confess it's true.
Lucifer:	Then you must know my words are true. I know that this life of yours as a hermit is not your true life. If you follow my advice your life can change and I will give you all your dreams' desire. At the end of this journey, these shepherds will have no more than they began with. The Messiah you go to see is a deceiver sent by the infernal fallen angels to trick holy men such as yourself. If you return with me, you will one day see the true Messiah. Until that blessed time, you will live a life of riches and splendor.
The Hermit:	(*Tempted by Lucifer's words.*) Give me a sign that your words are true.
Lucifer:	I will be your best friend, and I will hold you close in my arms. See the shepherdess sleeping over there?
The Hermit:	Yes.
Lucifer:	Just as I looked into your soul and saw your dreams, I have looked into hers, and I know that if you go take her hand, she will leave with you, and you two shall be married.
The Hermit:	She wants to marry me?!
Lucifer:	It is true. Just go and take her hand and leave with her. I am here by your side, and soon you shall have the life you deserve, with me and the shepherdess by your side.

(*The Hermit falls for Lucifer's temptations. Sneaking cautiously over to Gila, he takes her by the hand and tries to leave with her.*)

Lucifer:	(*Yelling.*) ¡*Pastores!* Wake up! The hermit is trying to steal the innocence of Gila!

(*The Hermit is so shocked by this turn of events that he freezes, motionless, holding onto Gila.*)

Gila:	(*Trying to shake loose the Hermit's grip.*) Bato! Tebano! Gil!
Bato:	(*Waking up.*) What is it, Gila?

From ¡*Teatro! Hispanic Plays for Young People.* Copyright © 1996. Teacher Ideas Press. (800) 237-6124.

Gil: | (*Leaping to defend Gila.*) You evil hermit!

(*The Shepherds free Gila and begin to beat the Hermit. Lucifer stands to the side, enjoying the chaos he has created.*)

The Hermit: | *Pastores*, listen to my story!

Bato: | What do you have to say, hermit.

The Hermit: | (*Trying to explain his actions.*) There was a man here while you were sleeping. He tempted me with riches and the promise of a life of splendor. He told me that Gila wanted to marry me. And that is why I was trying to leave with Gila.

Gil: | The man was *El Diablo*.

The Hermit: | I have committed a million sins. Please forgive me, *pastores*.

Bato: | That is why we are on this holy journey to *Belén*. The Redeemer is born to save us from the temptations of *El Diablo*.

The Hermit: | Listen, *pastores*. Listen to the heavenly voices that are once again coming to us.

(*Angel enters.*)

Angel: | *Pastores*, the Savior is born. You are invited to the blessed stable in *Belén* to witness the holy miracle of the birth of the Christ Child.

Bato: | The heavens have sent us a reminder not to follow the path of temptation and to continue our holy journey. *Pastores*, let us gather our belongings and follow the brilliant star to *Belén*.

Lucifer: | What is this music that causes me so much pain. My bitterness becomes greater, and my rage is more painful with each sound from the heavens. But now my revenge begins. These shepherds shall die before they see their Redeemer.

(*Lucifer approaches the Shepherds. When they see him approaching, they cower in fright. Suddenly, the Angel appears, accompanied by the Archangel Miguel.*)

Angel: | I have more joyful news for you, *pastores*. I bring the Archangel Miguel from the brilliant heavens to do battle with *El Diablo*.

Archangel Miguel: | (*To Lucifer.*) Tell me, deadly serpent, who are you after with your evil temptations?

Lucifer: | *Los Pastores.*

From *¡Teatro! Hispanic Plays for Young People*. Copyright © 1996. Teacher Ideas Press. (800) 237-6124.

Archangel Miguel:	I am here to defend them. And I will crush you and send you back to your fiery caverns for all eternity. *Pastores*, to you I bring the true news that in *Belén* is born the Redeemer of life, the King of heavens and the earth.
All Shepherds and the Hermit:	*¡Que viva!*
Lucifer:	Miguel, you have always been my adversary. But today I will reign supreme. My power will rule over you and the earth.
Archangel Miguel:	With the powers of heaven I will defeat you.
Lucifer:	It is impossible to defeat me!
Archangel Miguel:	I am the defender of the Eternal Father.
Lucifer:	And I am the power from whom all evil spreads. Draw your sword, helpless defender.

(They draw swords and begin to fight. The battle is even at the beginning, but soon it becomes clear that the Archangel Miguel will win. As the battle continues, Lucifer begins to lose strength until he is finally defeated and lies under the foot of the Archangel Miguel.)

Archangel Miguel:	The Prince of Darkness is defeated! And now, cursed one, I must destroy your very breath. Surrender your sword. *(He takes Lucifer's sword.)*
Lucifer:	Cursed be my violent envy.
The Hermit:	Evil master, you have fallen at the feet of the Archangel Miguel. Did you really think your evil would last forever?
Archangel Miguel:	He fell from high because he was disloyal and proud.
Lucifer:	But I am the fearless Lucifer.
Archangel Miguel:	Your fall is a lesson for everyone.
Lucifer:	Dear little flowers, learn from me how different yesterday is from today. Yesterday I was a marvelous being. Today I am not even a shadow of myself. The redemption has arrived and I have been defeated.
The Hermit:	How do you like it, Lucifer? Now that you are held in the power of the Archangel Miguel.
Archangel Miguel:	Let the swords clang with great fury. Lucifer has lost. Get up, horrid beast, and bury yourself in the eternal flames. God has condemned you and has given humanity the powers to fight your temptations. Open your pits, eternal flames, and receive your master.

(The Archangel Miguel exits with Lucifer.)

From *¡Teatro! Hispanic Plays for Young People.* Copyright © 1996. Teacher Ideas Press. (800) 237-6124.

Angel:	Go *pastores*, lovingly seek the Child of *Belén*. (*Angel exits.*)
Bato:	The heavens sing victory because the Archangel Miguel has won. What a beautiful night! *Pastores*, our lives have been saved. Let us go find the Christ Child in his stable and give thanks.
Gila:	(*Shaking Bartolo who has slept through all the events of the nights.*) Bartolo, get up! Let us go see the newborn King.
Bartolo:	(*Trying to stay sleeping.*) You go see him for me. Your manners are better than mine anyway.
Gila:	Bartolo! Don't be so lazy!
Bato:	Bartolo, you have to get up and come with us to *Belén*.
Bartolo:	Go if you want to go. I don't want to go. I just fell asleep.
Tubal:	Bartolo, even the donkeys and oxen are there.
Bartolo:	If it is a donkey, it could kick me.
Tetuán:	The stars are pretty high, Bartolo. It's time to get up.
Bartolo:	Just when I was beginning to sleep, you come and disturb me.
Gil:	Get up, Bartolo. Don't be so lazy!
Bartolo:	I have rested enough on this side. I will try the other side now. (*He turns over.*)
Bato:	Bartolo, the morning star has risen.
Bartolo:	Really, I just heard the evening bells.
Gila:	Bartolo, *La Gloria* is in *Belén*.
Bartolo:	If *La Gloria* wishes to see me, then let *La Gloria* come to me.
The Hermit:	(*Temptingly.*) There is chocolate in *Belén*.
Bartolo:	Good, bring me some on the way back.
Gil:	There is food in *Belén*.
Lépido:	There is wine and drink in *Belén*.
Bartolo:	You know, maybe it is time to get up and go. Give me your hands to help me rise so I do not fall. (*The Shepherds help him get up.*)
All the Shepherds, except Bartolo:	Finally!

From ¡*Teatro! Hispanic Plays for Young People.* Copyright © 1996. Teacher Ideas Press. (800) 237-6124.

Bartolo:	(*Looking sadly at his bedsite.*) I'm sorry I have to leave you, little bed. Good-bye.
Bato:	Now we are ready! Do you all have a gift for the Christ Child? I am giving Him these little charms filled with my love.
Tebano:	I am giving my sheepskin I made as a gift to heaven.
Gil:	I also am giving a wool fleece to keep Him warm on this wintry night.
Lépido:	I have saved a small altar cloth. With great humility I will offer my gift.
Tubal:	This honeycomb will be my gift to the Holy Child.
Tetuán:	I have made a cradle. Strong and beautiful. A holy resting place for the newborn Redeemer.
The Hermit:	I am giving my book of prayers to the Child. They have given me strength through these thirty years and have brought me to this holy place.
Gila:	And I am giving these crystal jewels and my heart above all.
Bato:	And Bartolo, what are you giving the Christ Child?
Bartolo:	I have been sleeping so much I don't know. But when we get there, I will give my adoration and prayers.
Bato:	*Pastores*, let us go with great joy singing holy verses. The brilliant star of *La Noche Buena* will lead us. The Redeemer is waiting for us in his holy manger.

(*All exit.*)

Scene 4: In Bethlehem before the manger.

(*The Shepherds and the Hermit enter, quietly and respectfully with their gifts.*)

Bato:	The Child is sleeping. Let us show our great joy and merriment without waking Him. Let us sing a lullaby.
The Hermit:	Oh beautiful Child, I wish to thank you a thousand times for your great victory.
All:	Sleep, beautiful Child. Sleep while choirs of angels sing to you. Of Herod you shall have no fear. Safe in your mother's arms, there's nothing at all that can harm you. Sleep, beloved child, tender and dear.
Gila:	Now we have adored the Child. We will leave this holy place filled with heavenly joy.

(*All step forward and place their presents by the manger.*)

From *¡Teatro! Hispanic Plays for Young People*. Copyright © 1996. Teacher Ideas Press. (800) 237-6124.

All: Good-bye, Jose. Good-bye, Maria. Good-bye, beloved Child. The shepherds are leaving filled with peace and love. Give your blessing to all of us, including the hermit. Give us life and health so that we may return next year.

(*All exit.*)

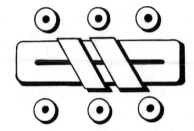

From ¡*Teatro! Hispanic Plays for Young People.* Copyright © 1996. Teacher Ideas Press. (800) 237-6124.

Part
IV
An Historical Play

La Batalla de Cinco de Mayo
The Battle of Cinco de Mayo

Introduction

Cinco de Mayo, or the 5th of May, is a holiday celebration of the victory of the Mexican army over the French invaders at the Mexican city of Puebla on May 5, 1862. The battle is significant because the outnumbered Mexican forces defeated a French army that was considered the most powerful in the world at the time of the battle. Also, the victory was an important moment of opposition to the French aspirations to set up an extension of its empire in the Americas.

In 1862, Mexico had recently created a republican form of government and elected its first president, Benito Juárez. Many conservative Mexicans, however, were not in agreement with the idea of a republican form of government, and they created political unrest in the country and sought supporters in Europe for their efforts to change the government of Mexico back to a more conservative rule. At the same time, France was seeking an opportunity to establish an extension of its empire in the Americas. Knowing that the United States was occupied with its own civil war, France sent an invading force to set up a French presence in Mexico.

France sent its best-trained and best-equipped troops, under the command of a famous general, to what they thought would be an easy conquest of Mexico. The under-manned and under-equipped Mexicans, however, valiantly fought the French at Puebla and, in a stunning military victory, defeated the French. The French Emperor Napoleon III was so incensed by the Mexican victory that he sent 30,000 additional French troops to Mexico. Overwhelmed by this massive French military force, the Mexicans were eventually defeated, and Benito Juárez had to flee Mexico City. The French did rule Mexico for five years. In 1867, however, Benito Juárez and his Mexican-loyalist followers finally succeeded in defeating the French and, once again, established Mexico as an independent nation.

The Battle of Puebla was an important historical moment for the new country of Mexico. The victory of the Mexican forces over the French forces became a symbol of Mexican pride and national fortitude. Through the years, the holiday of *Cinco de Mayo* has evolved from just a memorial of an important historical event into a more encompassing celebration of cultural pride and accomplishment.

Though the scenes of this play are fictionalized, the events dramatized in the play are historically factual and accurate. The characters and events depicted in the play are based on historical accounts of the *Cinco de Mayo* battle. Each scene is designed to convey an important historical set of facts representing the events leading up to and causing the Battle of Puebla. The statements and political positions taken by the principal characters are based on historical records and interpretations of historical events.

Staging

The scenes of this play are all interior scenes. Simple arrangements of furniture will indicate these interior locations.

Props

None necessary.

Costumes

See figure 9 in the introduction to this book.

Cast of Characters

The Narrator

Benito Juárez, *President of Mexico*

General Ignacio Zaragoza, *leader of the Mexican armies*

General Miguel Negrete, *a Mexican General*

General Colombres, *a Mexican General*

General Arratia, *a Mexican General*

General Rojo, *a Mexican General*

General Porfirio Díaz, *a Mexican General*

General Charles Latrille, *leader of the French armies*

General Juan Almonte, *the conservative Mexican Ambassador to Paris*

General Haro, *a conservative Mexican General*

Napoleon III, *Emperor of France*

General Doblado, *the Mexican Secretary of State*

Commodore Dunlop, *the British envoy*

Jean Pierre Dubois, *the French Ambassador*

General Juan Prim, *a Spanish General*

Mexican official #1

Mexican official #2

French official

Scene 1: The office of newly elected Mexican President Benito Juárez.

The Narrator:	The nineteenth century was a time of great historical importance for the new nation of Mexico. Mexico, known as New Spain during the Spanish colonial period, did not become an independent country until 1821. Mexico's independence day, similar to the United States' July 4th celebration, is September 16th. That date commemorates the famous day in 1810 when a priest, Father Miguel Hidalgo y Costilla, set into motion the series of events that would lead to Mexico becoming its own independent country, no longer subject to Spanish rule. After its independence, Mexico tried several forms of government, from dictatorship to monarchy. During this time, the new nation of Mexico suffered from great civil strife and economic struggle. During this time it also lost a disastrous war with the United States in which it lost half of its land to the United States. Finally, in 1857, Mexico established a government based upon democracy. Benito Juárez became Mexico's president and assumed the leadership of an economically bankrupt county torn apart by years of internal hostilities. At the beginning of his term of office, President Juárez faced many difficult decisions.

(*Juárez and two Mexican officials enter.*)

Official #1:	President Juárez, we have received notice from Spain, England, and France that they demand payment of our foreign debt.
Official #2:	It can't be a serious demand. They must realize that we are a new government of a country with no economic resources. Even our silver mines that, in the past, served as a source of income are no longer in production.
Official #1:	If only the previous governments had realized the mines' economic importance and had not neglected the mining industry, we could now use the income from silver to pay these foreign debts.
Juárez:	But that is all wishful thinking. The facts are that Mexico's economy is bankrupt and that our country doesn't have the money to pay these debts.
Official #1:	There is word that they are going to invade Mexico.
Juárez:	Preposterous! Mexico is no longer a colony up for invasion and conquest. We are an independent nation recognized in the world community.
Official #1:	Mexican conservatives have been in France trying to gather support to overthrow your government, President Juárez.
Juárez:	Who has been doing these treasonous acts against the elected government of Mexico?

From ¡*Teatro! Hispanic Plays for Young People.* Copyright © 1996. Teacher Ideas Press. (800) 237-6124.

Official #2:	General Almonte is trying to convince the French court that it should establish itself in Mexico and return the country to conservative rule.
Juárez:	We will fight to the death all efforts to invade our country.
Official #1:	France is using our nonpayment of the foreign debt to her as a just cause for invasion.
Juárez:	What is the debt to the three countries?
Official #1:	The debt to England is almost 69 million *pesos*. The debt to Spain is almost 10 million *pesos*. The debt to France is 2 million *pesos*.
Juárez:	The debt to France is the smallest of all. It is almost insignificant compared with the debt to England. And yet France is the most demanding.
Official #1:	Almonte is behind this.
Official #2:	He has convinced Napoleon that we should be invaded.
Juárez:	There is only one course of action for us. We will have to declare a payment moratorium on all domestic and foreign debt for a period of two years. This will give us time to build and strengthen our economy.
Official #1:	The countries will still demand payment.
Juárez:	We will assure our world partners that we will religiously resume payments when circumstances allow it. These are agreements countries make in situations such as this one.
Official #2:	We will have to have Congress vote on the moratorium.
Juárez:	That is required by our new democratic constitution.
Official #1:	I don't think the French will agree to it. Almonte and his followers are determined to overthrow this government and they have the ear of the French Emperor.
Juárez:	These forces threaten the very survival and existence of our democratic government. War seems inevitable, and Mexico is worth a battle, but we must do everything we can to avoid one.

(*All exit.*)

Scene 2: France, the court of Napoleon III.

The Narrator:	The Mexican Congress voted and supported the debt payment moratorium by a vote of 1,112 to 4. The moratorium was a democratic decision supported by the elected Congress of Mexico. This decision was vigorously attacked by the Mexican conservatives in Europe. At the court of the

From ¡*Teatro! Hispanic Plays for Young People*. Copyright © 1996. Teacher Ideas Press. (800) 237-6124.

French Emperor Napoleon III, Mexican conservatives have convinced the French to invade Mexico.

(*Napoleon, Almonte, and a French official enter.*)

French Official:	We have received word that Juárez is declaring a stop to foreign payments.
Almonte:	Mexico is politically weak. It is unable to pay these debts. Now is the time to establish France in the Western Hemisphere.
French Official:	Mexico is an independent nation. It is an act of war to invade a country and overthrow its elected government.
Almonte:	But Mexico itself has delivered to us a "just cause" for intervention by not paying its foreign debts.
Napoleon III:	Then we will invade Mexico and make it a part of France.
Almonte:	It is in Mexico's best interest that you invade and help establish a more conservative government.
Napoleon III:	The United States has declared the Monroe Doctrine, which states that no European government shall interfere in the affairs of the Americas.
Almonte:	The United States is right now deeply engaged in its own civil war, and it will not have the will or resources to oppose your intervention. You will have a clear path to Mexico City.
Napoleon III:	It is in France's best interest to invade Mexico. The United States has declared its Monroe Doctrine, but it has its own expansionist impulses. If it becomes the master of all of the Americas, it will be the only power from that area. But if a stable government is established in Mexico with French assistance, then we will have placed a dam to the expansion of the United States. It is our political and economic interests that compel us to march over Mexico and establish our flag.
French Official:	Juárez has vowed to defend Mexico.
Napoleon III:	France has the mightiest armies in the world. We will send our most experienced troops under the command of one of our most experienced generals. Mexico's efforts will be of no consequence.

(*All exit.*)

Scene 3: The office of Mexican President Benito Juárez.

(*Juárez and two Mexican officials enter.*)

Official #1:	France, Spain, and England have agreed to protect the life and property of their nationals and to obtain collection of their debts.

From *¡Teatro! Hispanic Plays for Young People*. Copyright © 1996. Teacher Ideas Press. (800) 237-6124.

Official #2:	The world press has criticized their positions but the three countries are united behind enforced collection, and they are preparing to invade.
Juárez:	What are the conservatives saying?
Official #1:	They are supporting the invasion. They see it as the opportunity they have been seeking to overthrow the government. Their newspaper *La Sociedad* has spoken in favor of the invasion and describes our democratic government as corrupted tyrants.
Juárez:	What is the state of the invasion?
Official #1:	Spain has prepared three divisions under the command of General Gutiérrez. The troops number more than 6,000 men. They have occupied the castle of San Juan de Ulúa and the port of Vera Cruz.
Official #2:	The French have sent nine companies of their most experienced African troops. The British have also occupied Vera Cruz.
Official #1:	They have delivered an ultimatum to the Mexican government: collection or intervention.
Juárez:	Then we have but one response to this invasion of our country. We will enact a law condemning to death all invading forces in Mexican territory.
Official #1:	President Juárez, that is declaring war against the invaders.
Juárez:	I call on all Mexicans to bury the hatred that has divided us and to unite in the defense of a greater and more sacred cause for all men and our people: the defense of the fatherland.
Official #2:	Is there no other course?
Juárez:	We will give peace one last chance. Send General Doblado to the village of La Soledad to try to reach one last compromise with the invading armies.

(*All exit.*)

Scene 4: Negotiations for peace.
In an office in the village of La Soledad.

(*As the narrator begins the scene, Doblado, Prim, Dunlop, Dubois, and Almonte enter. They set up in four distinct and separate areas on the stage. Almonte and Dubois are together in one area. The narrator moves from one group to the other as he/she discusses each event with each set of characters. The characters hold frozen, tableau poses until engaged in the scene.*)

From ¡*Teatro! Hispanic Plays for Young People.* Copyright © 1996. Teacher Ideas Press. (800) 237-6124.

The Narrator:	General Doblado met with representatives of the invading countries to negotiate a possible peace. Here we have Spanish General Juan Prim. He was the selected representative of the invading forces. Next we have General Juan Almonte, the Mexican conservative. He is with the French ambassador Jean Dubois. Finally, we have the British envoy Commodore Dunlop.
Doblado:	(*Speaking to Prim.*) Then it is agreed.
Prim:	Yes, we will sign the document known as the Agreement of *La Soledad.* In it we will recognize the government of Benito Juárez and the sovereignty of Mexico.
Doblado:	In turn, we will allow the invading troops to relocate from the yellow-fever-infected city of Vera Cruz. And we give you our government's assurances that Mexico will resume payment of its debt to your countries. (*He goes to Commodore Dunlop.*) Commodore Dunlop, the Mexican government has reached an agreement with Spanish general Prim, and we also give the British government our assurances that the Mexican government will resume its payments to England.
Dubois:	(*Speaking to Almonte.*) Doblado has assured the Spanish and English representative that it will repay its foreign debt.
Almonte:	The Emperor Napoleon has assured me that France is committed to a path of intervention. Even though Mexico's debt to France is by far the smallest debt, that debt is only a "just cause."
Dubois:	You are here under the protection of the French fleet, and you have been appointed dictator of Verz Cruz. In addition, there are Mexican conservative troops supporting the invasion.
Almonte:	Napoleon III is determined to overthrow the Mexican government and establish a French monarch in Mexico. He has selected the Austrian Maximilian von Hapsburg to be the monarch of Mexico.
Dubois:	He has placed General Charles Latrille as the commander of more than 6,000 French troops. With his thirty years of army service and eleven campaigns, he is one of France's most experienced and successful generals. We will use the same road to Mexico City that Cortéz used centuries ago to conquer Old Mexico. Our path is already determined.
Prim:	(*Speaking to Doblado.*) The Spanish government is satisfied with the Mexican government's assurances of repayment. We will withdraw our troops from Mexican land.
Dunlop:	(*Speaking to Doblado.*) Even though our debt is by far the largest, the English government is also satisfied with the Mexican government's assurances of repayment. We, too, will withdraw our troops from Mexican land.

From *¡Teatro! Hispanic Plays for Young People.* Copyright © 1996. Teacher Ideas Press. (800) 237-6124.

Dubois:	*(Speaking to Doblado.)* France does not accept the Mexican reassurances on the debt payments, and our intention is to establish a French monarchy in Mexico.
Doblado:	*(Speaking to Dubois.)* The French intentions are clear, and they leave Mexico no choice. The constitutional government, the guardian of the Republic, will meet force with force and shall wage war to the end, as justice is its cause.

(All exit.)

Scene 5: The City of Puebla.

The Narrator:	England and Spain did withdraw their troops from Mexico. France, however, continued its military march to Mexico City. Between the French and Mexico City stood the City of Puebla. The French General Charles Latrille was so confident in his army's military superiority and so dismissive of the Mexican defense that he made an arrogant statement that would come to destroy his military career.

(Latrille enters.)

Latrille:	*(Addressing the audience.)* We have over the Mexicans the superiority of race, of organization, of discipline, of morality and morale, and to further show our excellence, I say to our Emperor, that from this time, at the head of 6,000 soldiers, I am the master of Mexico. *(He exits.)*
The Narrator:	As the French approached Puebla, Mexican General Ignacio Zaragoza met with his generals to plan the defense of the city. One of his generals was Porfirio Díaz, who would one day become President of Mexico.

(Zaragoza enters with his generals—Negrete, Colombres, Díaz, Arratia, and Rojo.)

Zaragoza:	Generals, let me hear your reports on your preparations for battle. Today is May 4th and, as we speak, the French are preparing to battle tomorrow. I have already sent General O'Horan with 4,000 soldiers to meet the conservative forces sixty miles from Puebla and to block their advance.
Negrete:	Sending O'Horan with those forces leaves us with a smaller force than the French. We will be outnumbered.
Zaragoza:	Both our size and inexperience will be our greatest weaknesses tomorrow. But the traitorous conservative forces must not join with the French or our cause will be even more outnumbered.
Negrete:	But his troops include the best units of the Mexican cavalry.

From *¡Teatro! Hispanic Plays for Young People.* Copyright © 1996. Teacher Ideas Press. (800) 237-6124.

Zaragoza:	General Álvarez will command 500 riders in our defense. Their bravery and valor will teach the French about Mexican courage.
Colombres:	I have commanded troops to build fortifications around the forts of Guadalupe and Loreto.
Zaragoza:	We will make those forts the focus of our defense of Puebla.
Colombres:	We have fortified old churches and estates and we have dug trenches and constructed obstacles to the French troops. The forts are ready.
Díaz:	I will command an infantry division between the two forts. We will defend the forts with infantry and cannons.
Zaragoza:	Good.
Negrete:	I will occupy and defend the hills surrounding the forts.
Arratia:	My men and I are in place to defend Fort Loreto.
Rojo:	And I am ready to defend Fort Guadalupe.
Zaragoza:	Generals, now it is time to prepare the troops for the defense of our homeland. The resistance that this nation so far has offered is almost nothing. It is a shame that we have such a small contingent of troops to fight the foreign enemy. For this reason, we must all commit ourselves to die in our positions, because it is not logical to aspire for victory with such a small, ill-equipped army, but we shall inflict the greatest damage. Today you shall fight for something sacred. You shall fight for your Fatherland, and I promise you that this day's journey will bring you glory. Your foes are the first soldiers of the world, but you are the first sons of Mexico. They have come to take your country away from you. Soldiers, I read victory and faith on your foreheads. Long Live Independence! Long Live the Fatherland!

(*All exit.*)

Scene 6: Outside the City of Puebla at the French General Latrille's headquarters.

The Narrator:	Zaragoza and his generals were ready to defend their homeland. French General Latrille was also planning his attack on the fortifications at Puebla. But his reasoning was affected by his arrogance and his desire to demonstrate French superiority. His dismissal of the advice of Mexican conservative generals would spell his defeat.

(*Latrille enters with Mexican conservative generals Almonte and Haro.*)

From ¡*Teatro! Hispanic Plays for Young People.* Copyright © 1996. Teacher Ideas Press. (800) 237-6124.

Almonte:	General Latrille, we have learned that Zaragoza has built fortifications around the Forts of Loreto and Guadalupe. Also, Guadalupe is higher on a hill and will be more difficult to attack.
Haro:	Even though he has fewer men, these are very strong fortifications and they will be difficult to take.
Latrille:	I am anxious to show the world the superior military skills of the French troops.
Almonte:	It is our advice that you avoid Fort Loreto and Fort Guadalupe and that you attack from the southern and eastern flanks.
Haro:	They are less protected and offer the greatest chances of breaking through.
Latrille:	It does not matter where we attack. We are the greatest military force in the world. Our soldiers are professional, well equipped, well trained, and experienced in battle.
Almonte:	But Zaragoza is also experienced, and his troops have fought valiantly to defeat the conservative forces before. He has great power over his troops, and his men will fight to the death for him.
Latrille:	Well, this time he is facing French troops, not your Mexican troops. We also have the best military strategists, so I do not think that I will be needing your advice on how to win the battle. I have instructed Commandants Cousin and Morand to make a frontal assault on Fort Guadalupe. We will begin our assault tomorrow, the 5th of May.

(*All exit.*)

Scene 7: Cinco de Mayo.

The Narrator:	A Mexican conservative, Francisco Arangois, wrote: "The contempt of the French senior officers for the advice of Mexican conservatives has been the cause of many obstacles during this campaign." These words and the actions of the French General Latrille accurately describe the disregard the French had for all things Mexican. At 11 o'clock on the 5th of May, 1862, the Mexican forces began the defense of their homeland.

(*Zaragoza enters with Negrete.*)

Zaragoza:	The French have begun the attack.
Negrete:	Genera Zaragoza, the French are not attacking from the eastern flank of Puebla as we had anticipated. All our forces are arranged to defend an attack from the east.

From *¡Teatro! Hispanic Plays for Young People.* Copyright © 1996. Teacher Ideas Press. (800) 237-6124.

Zaragoza:	I sent Comandante Martínez and his sixty raiders of the cavalry battalion out to engage the French troops first, and I can tell by the dust in the sky from their horses that the French are attacking Guadalupe first.
Negrete:	It goes against all good military sense, but they are making a frontal attack on Fort Guadalupe.
Zaragoza:	Tell the generals to marshal their forces to defend Guadalupe! We fight for our families. We fight for honor. We fight for Mexico!

(*All exit.*)

Conclusion:

The Narrator:	(*Narrator enters and addresses the audience.*) The French had indeed decided to attack Fort Guadalupe. In his arrogance Latrille had decided to go for the dramatic victory and glory. His decision was built on the fact that he had never considered the possibility that the Mexican forces could win. Three times the French forces attacked Fort Guadalupe. Three times the Mexican forces fought back desperately. Three times the French forces had to retreat under heavy fire and sustained casualties. Realizing that he had been defeated, General Latrille ordered a full withdrawal of the French troops. On the 5th of May, 1862, at the City of Puebla, the Mexican forces defending their homeland from foreign invaders had defeated the mighty French forces. History records best what happened after the battle.

(*Juárez, Zaragoza, and Napoleon enter.*)

Zaragoza:	After the victory at Puebla, I wrote President Juárez. In this letter I wrote: "The French army has fought gallantly; however, its General has acted clumsily. On this long battle, the Mexican troops never turned their backs to the enemy. The armies of the nation have been covered with glory." (*He exits.*)
Napoleon III:	Defeated by the Mexicans! My plans stopped! This will not be. I will replace that disgraced Latrille with Supreme Commander Bazine, and this time I will send 30,000 troops! (*He exits.*)
The Narrator:	Napoleon did send 30,000 troops to Mexico and, a year later, he succeeded in placing Count Maximilian in Mexico city and establishing a French monarchy in Mexico.
Juárez:	In three years of dedicated battle, the loyal Mexican forces finally defeated the French once and for all. In 1867, the French left Mexico—and Mexico, once again, was an independent nation.

From *¡Teatro! Hispanic Plays for Young People.* Copyright © 1996. Teacher Ideas Press. (800) 237-6124.

The Narrator:	The victorious General Zaragoza never lived to see his beloved Mexico free. A few months after his mighty effort, General Zaragoza died. To commemorate this valiant General, Mexico renamed the city he defended with his life, *La Ciudad de Puebla de Zaragoza,* the City of Puebla-Zaragoza. Even the French came to admire the unbreakable will of the Mexican soldiers. In 1863, a Paris newspaper wrote: "The defense of Puebla-Zaragoza was one of the greatest in the history of warfare." President Benito Juárez's famous quote summarizes the historic efforts of the Mexican forces at the Battle of Puebla-Zaragoza on *Cinco de Mayo.*
Juárez:	Between two individuals as between nations, respect for another's rights is Peace!

From *¡Teatro! Hispanic Plays for Young People.* Copyright © 1996. Teacher Ideas Press. (800) 237-6124.

Glossary of Spanish Words

abuelita—a term of affection for "grandmother"

abuelos—grandparents

adiós—good-bye

agua—water

águila—eagle

arroz con leche—rice pudding

arroz con pollo—chicken with rice

Belén—Bethlehem

biscochitos—anise-flavored cookies

buenos días—good day, good morning

burrito—a rolled tortilla, usually filled with beans and meat and covered with green chili

calabacitas—zucchini with onions

calaveras—skeletons

Calavera Catrina—a very famous skeleton image of a grinning woman wearing a large decorated hat

chorizo—sausage

compadres—technically, the godparent of one's child; more commonly, a very close friend

conchero—a dancer who performs the traditional Aztec dances

copal—a resin incense

cuetlaxochitl—Aztec name for poinsettia

curandera—healer; a person who has the knowledge of the healing powers of plants and natural substances

dichos—proverbs

Dios—God

Doña—a formal form of address for "Madam" or "Mrs."

Don—a formal form of address for "Sir" or "Mr."

Duende—mischievous wandering spirits or dwarfs. The legend of the *Duendes* is that after the Lord and the devil had their arguments at the beginning of time, some of the angels stayed with the Lord and some went with the devil. When the Lord closed the doors to heaven and the devil closed the doors to hell, many angels were caught between heaven and hell with no place to go. These angels came to earth and became the *Duendes*. The *Duendes* spend their time causing mischief in human affairs.

El Diablo—the devil

elote—corn

empanaditas—fried, stuffed turnovers

familia—family

farolitos—a New Mexican Christmas season decoration made by filling paper bags with sand and lighting a candle placed in the sand.

fiesta—celebration

frijoles—beans

gato—cat

gloria—heaven

incensario—incense burner

jita—daughter; a term of affection from a parent to a child

jito—son; a term of affection from a parent to a child

la noche buena—the good night, Christmas Eve

la misa del gallo—midnight mass on Christmas Eve. Literally translated as the "mass of the rooster" because, in the old days, the mass lasted so long that people heard the roosters on the way home from the mass.

león—lion

loco—crazy

los ancianos—the old ones; the elders

los angelitos—little angels

lumbre—fire

luminarias—another name for New Mexican Christmas-season decorations made by filling paper bags with sand and lighting a candle placed in the sand; also the term for a small bonfire

madre—mother

mamacita—mom

mi—my

milagro—a miracle

nube—cloud

ofrenda—an offering or gift; an altar decorated with offerings or gifts

oso—bear

padre—priest; father

palito—little stick

pan de muerto—bread of the dead

papel picado—cut paper; paper cut-outs

pared—wall

pastores—shepherds

perro—dog

peso—the basic Mexican monetary unit

posada—an inn

posole—hominy stew

que viva—hurray

ratón—mouse

señora—married woman or an elder woman

señorita—unmarried woman or a young woman

señor—sir; Mr.

sí—yes

sol—sun

sopaipillas—fried, puffed bread

tamale—a traditional Mexican food of meat and chile mixed inside a corn meal dough and wrapped in corn husks

tecolote—owl

tia—aunt

tilma—a poncho

tio—uncle

tortilla—the staple bread of Mexico. A flat, round white flour bread

tripitas—intestines

vamos a comer—let's eat

viejito—old man

viento—wind

Bibliography

Aranda, Charles. *Dichos: Proverbs and Sayings from the Spanish*. Santa Fe: Sunstone Press, 1977.

Brown, Lorin W. *Hispano Folklife of New Mexico*. Edited by Charles L. Briggs and Marta Weigle. Albuquerque: University of New Mexico Press, 1978.

Cabello-Argandoña, Roberto. *Cinco de Mayo: A Symbol of Mexican Resistance*. Encino, CA: Floricanto Press, 1993.

Campa, Arthur L. *Hispanic Culture in the Southwest*. Norman: University of Oklahoma Press, 1979

Cobos, Rubén. *Refranés: Southwestern Spanish Proverbs*. Santa Fe: Museum of New Mexico Press, 1985.

Cortes, Carlos E., ed. *Hispano Culture of New Mexico*. New York: Arno Press, 1976.

Espinosa, Aurelio, and J. Manuel Espinosa, eds. *The Folklore of Spain in the American Southwest: Traditional Spanish Folk Literature in Northern New Mexico and Southern Colorado*. Norman: University of Oklahoma Press, 1985.

Espinosa, José Manuel. *Spanish Folktales from New Mexico*. New York: American Folklore Society, 1937.

Everts, Dana L. *Tradiciones Del Valle, Folklore Collected in the San Luis Valley*. Edited by Mark V. Dalpiaz and Dana L. Everts. Alamosa, CO: Rio Grande Arts Center, 1986.

Huerta, Jorge. *Chicano Theatre: Themes and Forms*. Tempe, AZ: Bilingual Press, 1982

Kanellos, Nicolás, ed. *Mexican-American Theatre: Then and Now*. Houston: Arte Público Press, 1983.

Philippus, M. J., and John F. Garcia. *The Two Battles of Cinco de Mayo*. Denver, CO: Education Foundation, 1990.

Rosenberg, Joe, ed. *¡Aplauso!, Hispanic Children's Theatre*. Houston: Arte Público Press, 1995.

Salinas-Norman, Bobbi. *Indio-Hispanic Folk Art Traditions, vols. I and II*. Albuquerque: Piñata Publications, 1987.

Stark, Richard. *Music of the Spanish Folk Plays in New Mexico*. Santa Fe: Museum of New Mexico Press, 1969

Tushar, Olibama López. *The People of El Valle, A History of the Spanish Colonials in the San Luis Valley*. Pueblo, CO: El Escritorio, 1992.

Vigil, Angel. *The Corn Woman: Stories and Legends of the Hispanic Southwest*. Englewood, CO: Libraries Unlimited, 1994

Weigle, Marta, and Peter White. *The Lore of New Mexico*. Albuquerque: University of New Mexico Press, 1988.

West, John O., ed. *Mexican American Folklore*. Little Rock, AR: August House, 1988.

About the Author

Angel Vigil is Chairman of the Fine and Performing Arts Department and Director of Drama at Colorado Academy in Denver. He is an accomplished performer, stage director, and teacher. As an arts administrator, he has developed many innovative educational arts programs for school and art centers.

Angel is an award-winning storyteller. His awards include the Governor's Award for Excellence in Education, a Master Artist Award and a COVisions Recognition Fellowship from the Colorado Council on the Arts, and the Mayor's Individual Artist Fellowship from the Denver Commission on Cultural Affairs.

Photo: Jan Pelton

Angel is the author of *The Corn Woman: Stories and Legends of the Hispanic Southwest*, selected as one of the 1995 Books for the Teen Age by The New York Public Library. He also cowrote *Cuentos*, a play based on the traditional stories of the Hispanic Southwest. He is featured storyteller on *Do Not Pass Me By: A Celebration of Colorado Folklife*, a folk arts collection produced by the Colorado Council on the Arts.

from Teacher Ideas Press

Other Related Titles

THE CORN WOMAN: Stories and Legends of the Hispanic Southwest
Angel Vigil

The culture, history, and spirit of the Hispanic Southwest are captured for readers in this sumptuous collection of 45 myths, legends, and original contemporary works. Fifteen stories are also presented in Spanish. An engaging way to learn or reinforce understanding of the rich Hispanic heritage. **All levels.**
World Folklore Series
xxxi, 234p. color plates ISBN 1-56308-194-6

THE CORN WOMAN: Audio Stories and Legends of the Hispanic Southwest

A wonderful supplement to story hour, these selected tales from the book are available in either English or Spanish. Of course, they are great for Spanish-language classes.
Eng. (approx. 60 min.) Order# A946: Span. (approx. 60 min.) Order# B946
Set of both tapes (approx. 60 min. each) Order# X946

STAGINGS: Short Scripts for Middle and High School Students
Joan Garner

These original, skill-specific scripts were designed around the guidelines for the theatre discipline of the the National Standards of Arts Education. Simple and affordable to produce, the nine plays make up this resource that *Booklist* calls "A must purchase for drama and literature studies." **Grades 6–12**.
xiii, 233p. 8½x11 paper ISBN 1-56308-343-4

ARTSTARTS: Drama, Music, Movement, Puppetry, and Storytelling Activities
Martha Brady and Patsy T. Gleason

Selected as as an Editors' Choice by *Learning Magazine*, the material in this book makes it easy to integrate the arts into the classroom. Teachers and students alike love its lively approach and classroom-tested activities. **Grades K–6.**
xii, 219p. 8½x11 paper ISBN 1-56308-148-2

FRANTIC FROGS AND OTHER FRANKLY FRACTURED FOLKTALES FOR READERS THEATRE
Anthony D. Fredericks

More than 20 reproducible satirical scripts grab the attention of even the most restless or reluctant learner. Use these wacky stories to encourage reading or as a showcase for students to learn how to write their own scripts. Learning sneaks up on them while they're laughing! **Grades 4–8.**
xiii, 123p. 8½x11 paper ISBN 1-56308-174-1

AMAZING AMERICAN WOMEN: 40 Fascinating 5-Minute Reads
Kendall Haven
Foreword by Molly Murphy MacGregor,
Executive Director, National Women's History Project

These concise, action-packed reads detail the stories of some of the women who helped shape our nation. The stories are so enlightening and inspiring that some students have been known to read more about these heroes ON THEIR OWN. These short stories are great springboards for study across the curriculum. **All Levels.**
xxii, 305p. paper ISBN 1-56308-291-8

GREAT MOMENTS IN SCIENCE: Experiments and Readers Theatre
Kendall Haven

Significant moments and characters in the history of Western science come to life in 12 scripts that are linked with student experiments. These parallel or simulate the actual experiments in the stories, so that students can discover and learn the concepts for themselves. **Grades 4–9.**
xii, 227p. 8½x11 paper ISBN 1-56308-355-8

For a free catalog or to order these or any other titles, please contact:
Teacher Ideas Press/Libraries Unlimited • Dept. B11 • P.O. Box 6633 • Englewood, CO 80155
Phone: 1-800-237-6124, ext. 1 • Fax: 1-303-220-8843 • E-mail: lu-books@lu.com